COLLEEN J. PALLAMARY

Meet Bridgeport's Sweetheart Colleen J. Bartram

by

Colleen J. Pallamary

Pallamary Publishing

Pallamary Publishing
Ocala, FL
www.pallamarypublishing.com

First published by Pallamary Publishing May 25, 2017

ISBN 10: 0692893571 *(sc)*
ISBN 13: 978-0692893579 *(sc)*

Printed in the United States of America
North Charleston, South Carolina

This book is printed on acid-free paper made from 30% post-consumer waste recycled material.

Library of Congress Control Number: 2017907935

Book Jacket and Page Design: Matthew J. Pallamary/San Diego CA

For Mom

My Hero

My Inspiration

My Friend

COLLEEN J. PALLAMARY

ACKNOWLEDGEMENTS

The author would like to thank Matthew J. Pallamary for his support with this project and author Pete Peterson for his continued support and encouragement in all of my writing efforts. Special thanks to Lynne Engel-Holmes, Rachael Holmes, Crystal Griffin, Karen and Danny Mayer, Rita Knopf, and Maryellen Rivers for always supporting me with unconditional love and friendship. They are the sunshine in my life.

Much gratitude and love to Rose Marie Morash for being a true friend to Colleen Bartram Pallamary in later years when they both raised children in the tough streets of Dorchester, MA. during the turbulent 1960's. Marie always shared kind words and a loving heart during difficult times.

Last, but certainly not least, much admiration and gratitude to the solitary souls who tumble, fall, and get back up again bolstered by the strength of their own courageous spirits.

COLLEEN J. PALLAMARY

"The one who follows the crowd will usually get no further than the crowd. The one who walks alone is likely to find himself in places no one has ever been."

Albert Einstein

COLLEEN J. PALLAMARY

Introduction

What do cartoonist Al Capp, actor Robert Mitchum, and singer John Mayer have in common?

They are all from Bridgeport, a large industrialized city perched on the Pequannock River in Fairfield County, Connecticut. Originally home to the Paugusset Indian Tribe, the small fishing and farming community grew into a town, incorporated in 1821, then a city, incorporated in 1836. Famed circus promoter P.T. Barnum, born in Bethel, CT., adopted Bridgeport as his home, and over the years the city gave birth to flying Frisbees, S & H Green stamps, and Sikorski helicopters to name a few. Affectionately nicknamed "The Park City" in honor of their public park system, her industrious citizens made significant contributions to the state, nation, and world as part of their communal legacy. One of those talented people was a young girl named Colleen Joan Bartram and this is her story.

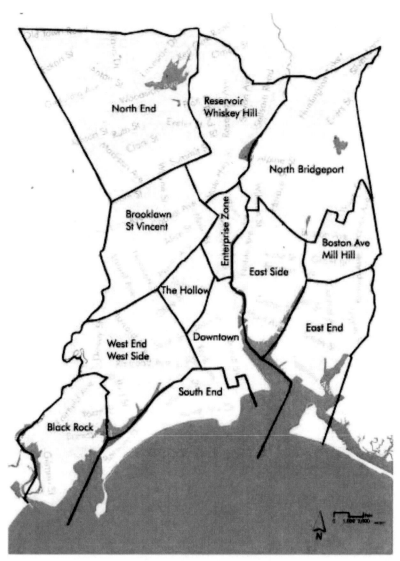

Map courtesy of Bridgeport.gov

Chapter One

At the beginning of the 20th century Bridgeport's population surge was fostered by a wide variety of work opportunities in the factories and blossoming businesses dotting the busy city streets. One of the many ethnic groups seeking jobs, religious freedom, and stability for their families were Hungarians who found support and guidance from their peers who had already settled in the city building bakeries, restaurants, and auto repair garages. Some were Romanian, others Slovakian, Austrian, or Ukrainian, but they all shared a common language and identified themselves as *Magyar*.

Weary immigrants were welcomed and put to work amongst family, friends, and neighbors, gravitating to the West End of Bridgeport. Some chose to move closer to Fairfield to escape the bustle of city life, among them Joseph and Mary Wargo one of many young Hungarian couples who immigrated to the United States in 1890 settling into an already established Hungarian community called "Hunk Town" by locals.

Walking through Hungarian neighborhoods, one could smell thick-crusted wheat bread (*Magyar kenyér*) baking in ovens, or glimpse greased pans covered in cotton cloth as the yeast fermented causing the dough to rise before baking in cast iron stoves. The unmistakable aroma of tender stuffed cabbage rolls simmering in cast iron pots and paprika-spiked Hungarian goulash bubbling in gravy greeted hungry factory workers as they ended their day.

Joseph Wargo found work as a molder in one of the many factories and over the years his loving wife Mary gave birth to several children. Sadly, not all survived. Their fourth child, a daughter named Margaret, learned at an early age that hard work and perseverance were cornerstones to survival and she worked and lived with relatives and family friends throughout much of her childhood, eventually finding work in a factory in downtown Bridgeport while in her teens. Margaret relied on her faith and resourcefulness to get by, attending Catholic mass on a regular basis and praying for guidance and strength for her family.

Sitting on the stoop outside the dingy factory during lunch break one day, she noticed a handsome, dark-haired man polishing the shiny hood ornament of a black Pontiac sedan parked outside the factory entrance. He returned each day at the same time waiting patiently for his passenger to finish whatever business he had inside the gray-walled building. She finally decided to wave hello if he happened to glance her way and he smiled at her the following week making her feel giddy with excitement for the rest of the day. After a few brief conversations they decided to meet for coffee one Friday afternoon and continued to see each other. The sight of the soft-spoken man towering over the diminutive factory worker became a source of gossip and giggles amongst Margaret's coworkers and friends.

Francis J. Bartram worked up the nerve to propose to his new love and on June 4, 1928, with her parents' permission and blessings, Margaret J. Wargo and Francis J. Bartram wed in Holy Trinity Church in the city of Bridgeport. He was 21 and she was 19.

Francis came from a long line of well-established Bridgeport natives who had lived within the city's boundaries for generations. His father William, a roofer by trade, married Mary Sheridan and Francis was the eighth child born to grieving parents who had already lost two other children at an early age. William was a skilled laborer who passed on his mechanical skills to his surviving sons. Francis, no stranger to hard work, helped his father lug wood and buckets of nails to job sites, marking and measuring asphalt shingles and planks of wood for whatever job was at hand. Marriage records indicate that Francis worked as a chauffeur and driving in town truly steered him toward his wife.

Francis and Margaret Bartram late 1920's

Chapter Two

In 1930, Bridgeport, like the rest of the nation, was entangled in the web of the Great Depression. The failing economy caused a domino-like effect on the lives and livelihoods of anxious citizens everywhere, but there were some community, church, and family-oriented events that brightened the outlook of the residents.

Colleen Joan Bartram was born on Sunday, May 25, 1930. Her slightly older toddler brother, Francis Jr., born in February of 1929, waited at home to greet his baby sister. Margaret and Frank had no idea that within five years the sleeping infant nestled in a soft cotton blanket at St. Vincent's Hospital would be tumbling and tap dancing her way into the hearts of Bridgeport's citizens.

Francis Sr., affectionately called "Frank" by his wife, bartered and scrambled for work both in and out of factories and eventually became an electrician, a much-venerated skill when electricity was being offered to rural communities for the first time. In a city filled with factories and munitions

17

plants, electricians were valued tradesmen.

While Frank worked long hours, Margaret, now called "Murph" by Frank, cared for her small children. Meager wages and the growing needs of children made mealtimes challenging. Some days the only meal available consisted of warm tea and leftover *Magyar* bread.

From 1930 through 1935 wages decreased and housing costs soared as a troubled nation dealt with a crumbling financial infrastructure. In 1930, the average annual wage was $1970 and the typical rental home was $15.00 a month. By 1935 the average annual income was $1600 and rents had increased to $22 per month creating a seesaw effect in wallets and pocketbooks. Reports of failing banks across the United States added to the weight of everyday living and the overall outlook for improvement looked grim.

Some form of respite from dismal news was desperately needed and that relief came via the blossoming entertainment industry. Radio, movies, and live performances provided troubled men, women, and children an affordable outlet to escape the harsh realities of everyday living and enabled them to engage in moments of illusion and fantasy even if only for a few minutes or hours each week. The evolution of the entertainment industry in the following years would have a huge impact on little Colleen Bartram.

Chapter Three

Radio City Music Hall opened in New York City in 1932 and the opulent venue instantly became a rousing success. Working class citizens now had access to the visual and aural splendor of live shows, exciting movie premieres, and, to the astonishment of star-struck fans, revered screen idols made dazzling personal appearances to publicize their latest work. Show business was evolving and a weary nation embraced it with open arms.

On special occasions Frank and Murph scraped enough money together to go an early matinee while relatives babysat. Glamourous stars like Bette Grable, Jean Harlow, and Bette Davis scorched the big screens with their smoldering beauty and sultry thespianism. Gangster movies with rugged leading men James Cagney, Paul Muni, and Edward G. Robinson rat-a-tatted their way across the country as the Prohibition era came to an end, and horror fans reveled at the sight of Boris Karloff's awkward gestures as *Frankenstein* (1931), Bela Lugosi's bloody fangs as *Dracula* (1931), and Boris Karloff again lumbering about swathed in tattered gauze as *The Mummy* (1932).

In 1933, while King Kong roared and Fay Wray screamed at the premiere of the movie at Radio City Music Hall, 5-year-old Shirley Temple signed a contract with 20th Century Fox studios. The following year she made her first film, *Stand Up and Cheer*, followed by *Bright Eyes* where she sang "On the Good Ship Lollipop", catapulting "America's Little Darling" into the hearts and minds of people everywhere. Young mothers took note of the talented youngster's singing and dancing skills and Murph was no exception – she was captivated by the sparkling persona and charisma of little Miss Shirley Temple.

Another small pleasure during the Depression Era was listening to the radio. Like many other families in Bridgeport, the Bartrams cheerfully gathered around their floor model tube radio waiting for favorite programs to begin. *The Shadow*, a popular serialized mystery series engaged listeners in imaginative, curious tales. Comedic half-hour programs led by rising stars Jack Benny, Fred Allen, and Groucho Marx drew laughter from listeners delighted with their witty dialogues and engaging banter. For the youngsters in the home, Uncle Don Carney ruled the airwaves every evening from 6:00 till 6:30 and his program influenced both children and parents alike, and Uncle Don had a significant impact on young Colleen Bartram's life.

Chapter Four

In August of 1934 the Bartram family welcomed a new member, daughter Audrey, the third and last member of the Bartram clan. She was sickly and during one of her checkups the pediatrician noticed her sister Colleen's slightly bowed legs and diagnosed the 5-year-old curly-haired child with rickets, a painful condition caused by a combination of Vitamin D deficiency and poor nutrition. Many children around the country were afflicted by the disease, including a young girl from Texas named Ann Miller who later rose to fame as a dancer and entertainer.

It is easy to understand why a non-communicable disease was spreading among the very young population. The typical family could not afford balanced meals and nutrition took a backseat to gnawing hunger pangs and childhood maladies. A typical meal in those times included fried potato peel sandwiches, corn meal mush, boiled cabbage or watery bean soup. Cold rice and milk was a favorite in the Bartram household and on birthdays and holidays Murph made a "Wacky Cake" using no milk or eggs for a thrifty dessert treat.

The consensus on treatment for rickets was exercise to strengthen weakened muscles and prevent further damage to developing joints and bones, and the most cost effective and practical way to achieve that was to dance. Popular, fun, and easy to learn, dancing helped children focus on a goal and Shirley Temple was the perfect role model.

Murph enrolled young Colleen in the Bessie Marie Reilly School of Stage Dancing several blocks from their apartment in downtown Bridgeport. Frank's sister Kitty helped with the fees and several aunts offered to sew costumes when needed for the many performances given at the school.

Older brother Francis gripped the wooden handle of Audrey's wicker stroller to the dance studio. Murph coached Colleen on how and what to say to her classmates and instructors and reminded her of how lucky she was to be able to attend dance classes. Colleen just wanted her knees to stop aching. Little Audrey, wrapped in light blankets and wearing a wide-brimmed sun bonnet, laughed and giggled at her older brother when he stuck his tongue out and made funny faces. Their weekly ritual became a nice break from the confines of the small apartment they lived in.

According to family lore, the Bartrams were thrilled when little Colleen quickly rose to the top of her class, pushing past any pain and discomfort in her aching legs. She was captivated by the cadence of

a heel-toe-shuffle in choreographed routines and
worked hard to synchronize her steps with the
sounds of recorded music. Ballet offered a more
disciplined approach to dancing and the painful *pointe*
technique of balancing on the tips of fully extended
toes was a crucial and challenging part of any routine.
Acrobatic tumbles and headstands rounded out the
class and Colleen diligently practiced her somersaults
and backflips under the critical eye of Murph who
demanded perfection and precision.

Colleen J. Bartram circa 1935/36 Bridgeport, CT.

TENTH ANNUAL RECITAL

of the

Bessie Marie Reilly
School of Stage Dancing

BESSIE MARIE REILLY

Certified Teacher of the Ned Wayburn Institute of Stage Dancing
Student-Teacher of the Vestoff-Serova School of Ballet

AT CENTRAL HIGH SCHOOL

SATURDAY EVENING   MAY 23, 1936

Accompanist, Helen B. Reilly

STUDIO	RESIDENCE:
306 Fairfield Avenue	66 Vine Street
Phone 4-9206	Phone 4-2470

Head Usher, Mary Elizabeth Fitzpatrick

ASSISTANT USHERS

Lilli Kibart	Eva Dabbs Meunier	Colleen Murphy
Regina Riordan	Marie Mossop Reed	Muriel Stevens
Jeanette Herlihy	Wanda Rosenthal Green	Winifred McGuinness
Sylvia Johnson	Mary Louise Brunetto	Margaret Chiota
Betty Balog	Nellie Zaccardi	Frances Hisam

PROGRAM

PART ONE

1. Let's Go! .... Baby Rose Marie and the "Scratle"
2. The Wedding of Jack and Jill .... Juvenile Tap Class
   Introduced by Grace Pinter

Jack .... Roger Resch
Jill .... Muriel Perry
Best Man .... William Resch
Maid of Honor .... Colleen Resnett
Minister .... Leonard Swanson
Ring Bearer .... Jean Riley
Train Bearer .... Barbara Thorp
Three Pigs .... Sandra Burghardt, June Dalbire, Josephine Behnen
Three Mice .... Georgiana Hoffman, Jean Bennett, Jean Ultrig
Little Boy Blue .... Clayton McDonagh
Old King Cole .... Robert Haeb
Farmer in the Dell .... Lorraine Fimn, Phoncia Demree, Mary Mihulik
Queen of May .... Dorothy Winters
Jumping Jack .... Vernon Sterner
Little Miss Muffet .... Catherine Resse
Cat and the Fiddle .... Betty Ann Dalkie
Farmer Girls .... Joyce Brand, Nancy Lou Reinhorst, Louise Smith
Carol Meade, Shirley Simmons, Mary Beth Crowe, Betty Gallagher
Bridesmaids .... Nancy Carman, Patricia McElroy, Norma Vitorelli, Gloria Aan
Milijhn, Eunice Herran, Jean Marie Stuart, Therese Marie Mellon

3. The Sugar Plums .... Virginia Chomp, Florence Tranchick

4. Effie Pranks .... Barbara Schneider, Beatrice Bodrue, Norma Jovino
   (They're always prancing in the forest each. Isn't a pair of shoes.)

5. You Hit The Spot .... They later find out they can Tap in them.)
   Leaders — Ellinor Sea, Margery Swanson .... Advanced Junior Tap Group

6. Two Neat Feet .... Muriel Nordstrom

7. Fur and Feathers .... Lillian Zolekos, June Hamon

8. Sweatin Like A Peacock .... Professional Tap Group
   Leaders — Pearl Schipice, Rose-Marie Voytek

9. Tippety-Tap .... Junior Tap-Tap Group
10. A Perfect Combination .... Doris Sorin, Lucy DeCoure
11. Walsot .... Clare Lowy
12. Curly Locks .... Elsie Tesh

PROGRAM

CONTINUED

13. School Days .... Junior Tap Group
    Teacher .... Mary Reed
    Leaders: Lorena Terry, Marion Gallagher, Gloria Crick, Rosemary Sterwich
    Girls: Patricia Rickel, Marion Amon, Jean Rose Jenliney,
    Marilyn Bruenwick, Barbara Schneider, Janet Davis, Mary-Lou
    McGuInness, Grace JMited, Shirley Liem
    Boys: Norma Jordan, Margaret Zuckerme, Fran Aaron, Dorothy Herma,
    Beatrice Bodrue, Grace Bneatoa, Jean Campbell, Catherine Larkin

14. Tears from Dixie .... Laura Linkowicz
15. Goody Goody .... Intermediate Tap Group
16. Happy Tip Toes .... Mae Brown
17. Ca Cincaracha .... Doris Smude, Olga Ungod, Doris Reinhardt
18. Our Nursery .... Senior Tap-Tap Group
19. Baby Sholks .... Tiny Grace Benteen
20. A Modern Quaker Maid .... Harrier Car Club
21. Soft Shoe Rhythm .... Mary Mason
22. Waltz Time Rhythm .... June Mary Voytek
23. Slow Leave .... Veronica Bender, Virginia Gray
24. The Snow Frolic .... Selected Ballet Groups
    a. Divertisement .... Peggy McCarthy, Rita Campbell
    b. Snow Fairies .... Juvenile Group
    c. Queen .... Colleen Resnett
    d. The Shepherd .... Professional Group
    e. Red and White Rhythm .... Junior Group
    f. Finale .... Professional Group

PART TWO

1. Acrobatic Demonstration .... Selected Group
2. Homemade Rose .... Shirley Finkelstein
3. Tea Tapping Toes .... Virginia Stevens
4. Whita Old Man .... Advanced Junior Tap Group
5. Goin' To Town .... Tiny Veroa-Ann Mahoney
6. Upstairs and Down .... Professional Roller Group
7. Let Yourself Go .... Sally McGuInness
   Before the Curtain — Catherine Kelly, Betty DeCoule
8. One Baby Grand .... Baby Rose Marie Frankhno
9. The Cod Pieh Roll .... Kindergarten Group
   Leaders — Bobby Haals, Chester McDonagh
10. Spills and Thrills .... Little Ethel Hkinck
11. Finnkink Tea-Tap .... Rita Campbell

Wacky Chocolate Cake

1-1/2 cup of all-purpose flour
3 tablespoons unsweet cocoa powder
1 cup granulated sugar
1 teaspoon baking soda
½ teaspoon salt
1 teaspoon white vinegar
1 teaspoon vanilla extract
5 tablespoons vegetable oil
1 cup water

Preheat oven to 350 degrees. Grease 8" or 9" round cake pan.

Add all dry ingredients to pan and mix. Make 3 depressions – 2 small and 1 large in dry mix. Pour vinegar in small depression, vanilla in other small depression and vegetable oil in large depression. Pour water over all and mix with fork till smooth. Bake for 35 minutes or until toothpick comes out clean.

Chapter Five

An anxious nation held its collective breath in 1937 when news reports chronicled the horrific explosion of the Hindenburg, a German passenger airship attempting to dock in New Jersey. Reports of the tragedy filled the airwaves and generated much speculation as to the cause. Not long after Amelia Earhart disappeared while on a flight across the Pacific Ocean, financial uncertainty weighed heavily on everyone's minds.

Caught in a social whirlwind of escapism via the entertainment industry, the focus for many shifted from societal woes to those magical moments when the voices and talents of people in both film and in person helped alleviate the stress of everyday living.

Little Colleen's extended family members on both sides were patriotic and civic-minded when it came to community efforts. Frank's ancestors included several Revolutionary War heroes and Murph's parents had made a new life for themselves despite the unrest and turmoil in their native Hungarian homeland. Families attended church together and communities worked hard to instill moral and ethical standards in the younger generation.

As part of her contribution to the well-being of those around her, little Colleen, known as "Bridgeport's Sweetheart", performed in a multitude of venues throughout the city, making weary people smile. She and other dancers proudly displayed their new dance skills while classmates and peers lay snuggled in warm blankets fast asleep in bed. Now a student at St. Joseph's R.C. School, Colleen worked hard to get good grades and practiced her dance routines in the crowded living room of her home while neighborhood children played outside.

The following is a partial list of performances documenting the blossoming career of a young girl who nursed bruised toes and aching muscles each night in her tiny bedroom while everyone slept.

Five Years Old

April 13-14, 1936
Bridgeport State Trade School – Sat evening
"Hit It Up" A John Rogers Production (part of ensemble)
May 23, 1936
Tenth Annual Recital Bessie Marie Reilly School
Central High School (several dance routines)

Six Years Old

December 5, 1936
Third Anniversary of Germania Turn Verein
Sat evening performance Acrobatic Dance

January 6, 1937
Minstrel and Dance   Wednesday Evening
Parishioners of Saint Raphael's R.C. Church Pyramid Mosque
Acrobatic dance performing with famed Baby Rose Marie

March 13, 1937
Park City Foresters of America Annual Dance &
Revue
(aka The Foresters 1937 Minstrel Company)
"A Night in Manhattan" Pyramid Mosque
Acrobatic Specialty

April 19, 1937
Minstrel and Dance   Monday Evening
Columbus Boys Assoc. Pyramid Mosque
Acrobatic Dance

May 21, 1937
Eleventh Annual Recital Bessie Marie Reilly School
Friday Evening   Pyramid Mosque   Several routines

Seven Years Old

Feb. 4, 1938
Orcutt Boys Club Sponsored by West Side Mother's
Club and Middle Junior Council
"The Gay Nineties" directed by Chris Wesche
Acrobatic Dance (no encores due to length of program
included in program listing)

March 24, 1938
"A Musical Portrait" presented by The Rambler Club of
the YMCA directed by Chris Wesche
Acrobatic Dance

April 25, 1938
Minstrel and Dance Columbus Boys Association
Monday Evening Pyramid Mosque Acrobatic Dance

April 27, 1938
Young People of St. Joseph's Church Weds Evening
"College Daze" A Minstrel Show Jack Quill Director
Pyramid Mosque   Acrobatic Dance

Eight Years Old

June 3, 1938
Dance Recital Bessie Marie Reilly School
Concordia Hall   Acrobatic Thrills

April 22, 1939
Swinging Doors Variety Minstrel and Dance
American Legion Drum Corps at Pyramid Mosque
Acrobatic listed as "Bridgeport's Little Sweetheart" on
program

May 18, 1939
Minstrel and Dance Societies of St. Joseph's R.C.
Church
Jack Quill Director   Acrobatic Dance

Nine Years Old

October 27, 1939
Minstrel and Dance given by Bridgeport Cadets
"Melody and Nonsense" at St. Stephen's Hall
Acrobatic Dance

Chapter Six

I t was clear to all her knew her that Colleen was talented above the norm. With each performance her popularity soared along with her skills and she became expert in tap, ballet, and acrobatic feats. One person who took special note of her outstanding performances was musical director, Chris Wesche, a man who recognized her innate ability and charisma and saw an opportunity to expand and her exposure by having her join the Boy's Club as a drum majorette, a move that not only benefited her, but was popular for the club. One newspaper account of her membership in the club made special note of the fact that she was "the only acrobatic drum major in the state."

Actual envelope (artist unknown) Circa 1941

Between nightly performances across the city and her duties as drum majorette young Colleen was quite busy. Photographs show her captivating smile and bouncing ringlets. She led many marching bands to victories in statewide contests giving cheering citizens great joy at her achievements. Her participation in fund raising events helped send the whole Drum Corps to the 1939 New York World's Fair, where her talents were on display to an international audience. She proudly twirled her silver baton and tapped danced her way into the heart of Bill Robinson, Mr. Bojangles himself. The local newspaper wrote:

A Clever Little Gal

"Eight-year old Colleen Bartram who has gained renown and title of "Bridgeport's Sweetheart" with her acrobatic performances around town, is proudly displaying the latest addition to her collection of celebrities' autographs…It's from Bill Robinson, the hoofer, who saw her perform impromptu at the World's Fair and called her into his dressing room to compliment her on the act…"

Mr. Bill Robinson aka "Mr. Bojangles"
Courtesy of Pinterest

The sights, smells, and sounds of the World's Fair were a dream come true for Bridgeport's Sweetheart, much like Disneyland or Epcot is to today's youngsters. Legions of people from around the world strolled through the exhibits, pavilions, and gardens of the sprawling fairgrounds. Women dressed in calf-length dresses and skirts walked along the streets and sidewalks in chunky, thick heeled shoes, hats placed carefully on coiffed hair while men dressed in slacks and neatly pressed shirts pointed out the gigantic statues and monolithic structures punctuating the landscape. Trams and buses carried curious tourists from place to place while drivers versed in the layouts of various venues carefully bobbed and weaved through the throngs of walkers and workers scattered along the thoroughfares.

Several ongoing live performances went on each day, including precision ice skating, swimming, and surreptitious topless dancing cloistered in an adult only section of the park. Many skits and plays were performed on both indoor and outdoor stages entertaining dynamic crowds with plenty of opportunities to rest and refresh in between. The Bridgeport Boy's Club took special care to see that their young majorette was able to visit the many wonders of the international showcase. Colleen would have been astounded if she knew that she would be performing in many of the countries whose exhibits she enjoyed during her time at the fair and her visit with the battleship USS California would end up touching her life in an unusual way.

*Bridgeport, CT. Boys Club Band circa 1940/41
With Bridgeport's Sweetheart Leading the Parade*

Colleen Bartram leading the way down Main Street
Bridgeport

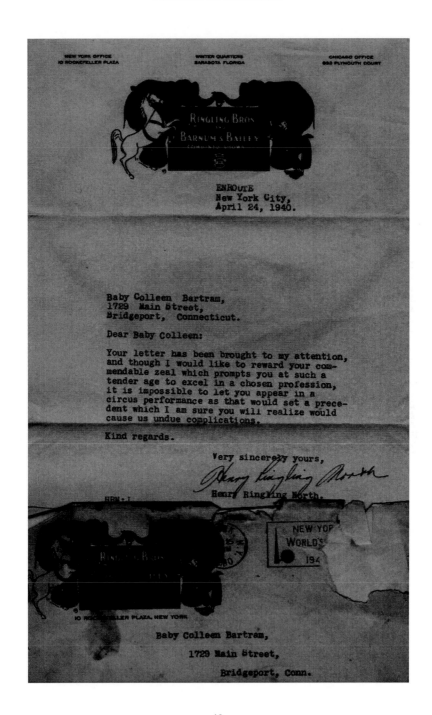

Chapter Seven

One of the biggest media personalities influencing both children and adults alike during the troubling tides of the Great Depression was Don Carney aka Uncle Don whose immensely popular children's program was broadcast every evening from 6:00 – 6:30 p.m. from WOR in New York City. Carney, once a vaudeville performer, understood the complexities of marketing, management, and money-making schemes and worked tirelessly to keep his own pockets lined with cash while making his program and presence an integral part of people's lives.

In his book, *Hi There Boys and Girls! America's Local Children's TV Programs (University Press of Mississippi ©️ 2001),* author Tim Hollis details the popularity and significant impact of children's programming throughout the years calling Uncle Don "the most famous local children's host in all of radio land."

Don was a pioneer in the radio industry. In his biography about Don Carney, *Head, Heart and Heel*

(Mayfair Books, Inc, ©1958), publicist and manager Bill Treadwell praised Don for being the first radio host to advertise a variety of sponsors instead of just one, as other programs did. Rather than pitch products on-air sight unseen, Don actually examined each item while on-air and then endorsed and recommended it to attentive listeners. His unorthodox approach to advertising made him popular with corporations and WOR, because families purchased whatever product he hawked that week.

Another ratings gimmick was the mention of birthdays for boys and girls. Children everywhere were stunned when Don, upon parental request, asked them to stop fighting with siblings or help around the house so they could be praised for good deeds. Grateful parents sent donations to the studio and praised the talents of Uncle Don. To young audience members, he was an omniscient relative floating through the speakers of floor radios everywhere. To parents he was a guidance counselor and role model, extolling the virtues of obedience and respect, truly a win-win for all.

In 1939 Uncle Don and station bigwigs decided to broadcast from the World's Fair in New York. A special studio was built in the New Jersey State Building and August 27, 1939 was declared "Uncle Don Day" as a way to celebrate his birthday amongst throngs of adoring fans. The popular host watched over six thousand children and adults participate in the bands and drum corps performances competing for prizes on the lawn of the New Jersey State

Building. According to Bill Treadwell it's very likely that Uncle Don cheered on the Bridgeport Boys Club led by a beaming Colleen.

After the success of the fair appearance, some sponsors felt uneasy about the fact that although regional products were accessible, there weren't enough national products available to children, the most valuable audience for his program. Local companies were still willing to participate, but certain formatting changes made it difficult, so it was time to reorganize and strategize a new approach for WOR and Uncle Don. Bill Treadwell took responsibility for the program changes implemented at WOR.

"For the perfect answer I set up the "Uncle Don Talent Quest". This gag utilized kids up to 15 in the WOR listening range of eighteen states, auditioning the hopefuls in the Mutual studios on Broadway and giving the winners a trip to California complete with screen test and possible movie role. The Santa Fe Railroad was contacted to zip the kids to the Coast, and they said fine. Hollywood movie studios also gave the green light. The chiefs at WOR said O.K., and got fully behind it. Finally, in homes miles from New York, thousands of stage mothers prepared to push Junior to stardom."
-excerpt from Head, Heart and Heel by Bill Treadwell

Murph Bartram was one of those stage mothers.

One of many promotional items for Uncle Don Carney
1940's.

Chapter Eight

A family friend urged Murph and Frank to enter their talented daughter in the widely publicized "Uncle Don Talent Quest". Her proven track record as a performer was a source of pride for the city of Bridgeport and her skills were undeniable. Murph's determination to capitalize on her young daughter's talent became a driving force in both their lives. With two other children to care for, Murph recognized the potential for financial gains in her daughter's budding career.

In 1941 Frank and Murph poured a cup of coffee and sat together at their oblong wooden kitchen table filling out the lengthy contest application Frank had picked up at the radio station. They placed a three-cent stamp on the envelope, dropped it in the mailbox, and kept their fingers crossed while waiting for a reply. If Colleen won there would be endless opportunities for the whole family to capitalize on the recognition and good fortune.

While her parents pored over the application, ten-year-old Colleen practiced each dance routine over and over, often late into the night. As if the rules and stipulations of the contest weren't intimidating enough, Murph's antics added an extra layer of stress to performances. Slaps and whacks on the head for minor mistakes were commonplace during practices and Murph's stern voice and countenance were all Colleen could see as she silently counted her moves in her head, twirling and tumbling on the wooden floors of their tiny apartment.

UNCLE DON
STATION WOR
1440 Broadway
New York City

"THE UNCLE DON HOLLYWOOD TALENT CONTEST

For children between ages of 8 and 15 years

"THIS APPLICATION MUST BE FILLED OUT AND READ

BY BOTH PARENTS (If you are child's legal guardian or if

One parent is dead, or child is orphan, please indicate at bottom

with signature).

NAME OF CHILD:

ADDRESS: *CITY:*

STATE:

AGE: *DATE AND YEAR*

OF BIRTH:

HEIGHT: *WEIGHT:*

SEX:

SCHOOL NOW ATTENDING:

PROFESSIONAL SCHOOLS:

DANCING, SINGING OR DRAMATIC SCHOOLS ATTENDED:

MOTHER'S OCCUPATION:

FATHER'S OCCUPATION:

WHAT PROFESSIONAL TRAINING

HAVE YOU HAD:
 ON WHAT RADIO PROGRAMS HAVE YOU APPEARED:
 ARE YOU UNDER CONTRACT TO ANY FIRM, PERSON, SCHOOL, OR ANY OTHER MANAGING AGENT:
 ARE YOUR PARENTS CITIZENS:
 THE FOLLOWING STATEMENT IS TO BE SIGNED BY BOTH PARENTS:

I, the undersigned, give as parents(guardians) my consent for the above mentioned child to partake of all the prizes offered by the Fifth Annual Uncle Don Hollywood Talent Contest and I also give my child permission to act and speak in whatever picture assignment is offered by this contest while the winners are in Hollywood on their annual trip. I also give my child permission to travel to Hollywood escorted by a member of Uncle Don's staff.

FATHER: *DATE:*
 MOTHER: *DATE:*
 ADDRESS: *CITY:*
STATE:
▪▪▪

"PRIZES: The two winners to be chosen sometime in April, will be taken to Hollywood on the Santa Fe Railroad with a representative of Uncle Don's office. After a tour of the picture studios, the children will return home.

FINALS: At the finals of this contest there will be about twenty judges from the theatrical field as well as picture company talent scouts. One boy and one girl will be chosen as the Most Talent Children in the Metropolitan Area. Several opportunities arise from this contest each year and Uncle Don reserves the right to announce these at a later date.

IN THE FINALS CONTESTANTS WILL BE JUDGED ON THE FOLLOWING:

PART ONE: Singing, dancing, or musical ability: general poise,

Presentation and selection of material.

PART TWO: Reading, diction and natural dramatic ability.

PART THREE: Physical appearance, hair, eyes, weight, height, teeth etc.

PART FOUR: Memory work, imitations or dramatic skit.

PART FIVE: Child will be asked a set of questions that boys and

girls their age should be able to answer.

Twenty points or parts thereof will be given for each **PART** listed above.

Eliminations will be held under the direction of Uncle Don's staff."

"At the first audition, children will be examined on **PARTS TWO, THREE** and **FIVE.**

If they pass this audition, they will be examined on the other two.

Quarter finals, semi-finals and finals will be held in March, 1942.

PLEASE NOTE: IMPORTANT: Childs birth

certificate must be presented when child takes first audition. No child will be permitted to be auditioned without it.

ADDRESS: *All auditions will be held at WOR, 1440 Broadway, New York City.*

Please report on the date listed above. Come on time. All must pass a diction test.

Entire contest under personal supervision of Uncle Don.

BILL TREADWELL *is the Director of Auditions.*

IF FALSE INFORMATION IS GIVEN, UNCLE DON RESERVES RIGHT TO REJECT CONTESTANT.

ALL CHILDREN MUST BE EIGHT YEARS OLD TO ENTER AND NOT OVER FIFTEEN YEARS AT TIME OF AUDITION."

(Excerpt from Head, Heart and Heel by Bill Treadwell © 1958)

Chapter Nine

Stage mothers made their presence felt on different levels. It was their responsibility to see that their child or children were transported to each venue on time, properly attired and ready to perform. They often stood in the wings behind long velvet curtains watching and critiquing every move and word of their stressed-out offspring. There were those who demanded, and often received, special treatment for their "shining stars." After all, they were the stars according to their Moms. Others sulked if they weren't given special recognition for simply making an appearance. Either way, promoters and producers alike were all too familiar with the quirky and obnoxious behaviors of parents who oftentimes lived vicariously through the actions of their innocent sons and or daughters.

Bill Treadwell and Uncle Don agreed that no parents would be allowed at Uncle Don auditions. They had both dealt with adults with overblown ideas of entitlement and made a stipulation that no parents were allowed, instructing the parents to drop off the child and return or wait outside while contestants vied for the winning prize.

On Friday, April 18, Colleen waited in the wings of the studio, butterflies dancing in her queasy stomach and Murph's criticisms echoing in her head. She tried not to wipe her sweaty palms on her costume and occasionally flapped her hands in the air to dry them off. She glanced at her feet to be sure her ankle socks were even and nervously tapped her toes to be sure she could hear the metal taps fastened to the soles of her polished shoes. The night before Murph had tugged and twisted the ends of her damp, golden-brown hair into pieces of torn cloth strips, rolling and tying each tendril into "rags", a popular styling technique used for centuries to produce long-lasting curls. In the morning, the bundles of cotton strips were untied loosening a cascade of tight ringlets around her face and slender shoulders. Murph wrapped each shiny curl around her index finger arranging her daughter's thick lustrous hair just so. Her handmade velveteen costume, adorned with gold trim, was carefully hung on the back of a chair to avoid wrinkles or tears. Polished white shoes were tucked beneath the same chair in the corner of her tidy room. Murph babbled directions and advice while her daughter sat and fidgeted waiting for the minutes to tick by.

She'd already warmed up that morning, stretching and bending gracefully into arched backbends, then reversing and touching her toes with outstretched fingers and straight legs, geometry-in-motion, shaping each move into dynamic forms that defied description. Her athleticism and poise, accentuated by her bright blue eyes and radiant smile charmed everyone whenever she performed.

Murph clutched Colleen's small hand in hers and led her to the entryway where contestants milled about. A huge **Contestants Only** sign hung on the studio door and Murph stopped, whispered a few words in her daughter's ear, then left. The nervous 68-pound acrobat exhaled deeply as she listened to her mother's high heels click down the hallway. A huge weight had just been lifted from her tiny shoulders. Knowing she wouldn't be subjected to Murph's critical remarks and icy stares made her less anxious and more confidant of her ability to perform. She smiled at the registrar seated at a desk and proudly pinned her identification number near her shoulder, careful not to wrinkle or mar her custom-made two-piece costume.

Chattering children gathered in the auditorium and watched their peers with longing in their hearts. From crooning to square dancing, the well- groomed contestants tried their hardest to impress the judges as the day wore on. Over 3,700 contestants had applied and Colleen was one of twenty-two who made the final cut. The judges were a mix of corporate sponsors who had arranged the perks and prizes for two young winners and Hollywood talent scouts keeping their eyes open for the next Shirley Temple or Mickey Rooney.

Colleen's hands shook and she breathed deep, reminding herself that Murph was not there to administer her usual verbal and physical punishments. She performed like a seasoned professional, bending, twirling, and standing on her head defying gravity with her style and grace. Fellow performers looked on in awe as she smiled, tumbled, and somersaulted her way to the top of the winner's list.

When all was said and done, Bridgeport's Sweetheart, Colleen Bartram, was declared the winner! Another winner was singer Gary Cole from New Haven, CT. and the wheels were in motion for them to go on an exciting adventure to Hollywood, where entertainment reigned supreme and publicity ruled the media.

Ready to go!

Nervous and waiting patiently for her turn.
Colleen Bartram 2nd left. 1941

Upside down and smiles all around!

Colleen Bartram 1941

Colleen Bartram Headstand 1941

Colleen Bartram Backflip 1941

Colleen J. Bartram **THE WINNER!!!**

1941 Winners Colleen Bartram and Gary Cole with
Uncle Don

Exciting Times! Colleen Bartram and Gary Cole 1941

FROM: JERRY DANZIG
WOR PRESS DEPARTMENT
1440 Broadway, New York

TWO CONNECTICUT YOUNGSTERS WIN
4TH ANNUAL UNCLE DON HOLLYWOOD CONTEST

It was a big day for the Nutmeg State at the finals of Uncle Don's Fourth Annual Hollywood ~~Talent contest to find the most talented boy and~~ girl in the Metropolitan area. The two winners are both from Connecticut - ten-year-old Colleen Joan Bartram of 1729 Main St., Bridgeport, and twelve-year-old Gary Cole of 80 Pardee Street, New Haven.

Over three thousand youngsters competed in the contest, twenty-two of them reaching the final audition which was held Friday (April 18) at the WOR Playhouse. Colleen and Gary will receive as their prizes a trip to Hollywood, with stop-overs at Chicago and the Grand Canyon, a chance to meet the stars and casting directors, a possible movie contract - and no school for a few weeks. The two children will leave for Hollywood on Sunday, May 4th.

One of the winners in last year's contest, Buddy Swan, plays Orson Welles as a child in "Citizen Kane."

EZRA STONE, HELEN MENKEN
ADDED TO BRITISH RELIEF SHOW

Helen Menken, Bert Lytell and Ezra (Henry Aldrich) Stone have been added to the all-star lineup for the "Young America Wants to Help" broadcast, under the auspices of the British War Relief Society, on WOR-Mutual this Sunday (April 27) from 11:30 a.m. to 12 noon.

Others taking part in this gala show are Helen Hayes, Gertrude Lawrence, Mayor La Guardia, the Yale Glee Club, the Youth Orchestra of New York City's High School of Music and Art. An original sketch by Moss Hart, a Ballad for Young American Voices, and original music by Kurt Weill, Pierre de Carllaux and Oscar Hammerstein will be featured.
4/21/41

WOR

BAMBERGER BROADCASTING SERVICE, INC · NEWARK, NEW JERSEY
NEW YORK BUSINESS OFFICE · 1440 BROADWAY, NEW YORK, N. Y.

FROM - - Bill Treadwell

SPECIAL PRESS RELEASE
* * * * * * * * * * * *

WINNERS IN THE UNCLE DON HOLLYWOOD TALENT CONTEST 1941

GIRL: Colleen Bartram   Age: 10
      1729 Main St. - Bridgeport, Conn.

BOY: Gary Cole Age: 12
      80 Pardee St. - New Haven, Conn.

It was a great day in New York Friday April the 18th. In the big New
Amsterdam Roof Theatre where there has been many a Ziegfeld hit, the
Fourth Annual Uncle Don Hollywood Talent Contest to pick the most
talented boy and girl in the Metropolitan Area was staged. This year
over 3769 children competed in the auditions for this trip to Hollywood,
a vacation at the El Tovar Hotel in the Grand Canyon, luncheon with
Mayor Kelly in Chicago, traveling first class on the Scout train of
the Santa Fe Railroad, and doing a special broadcast on WGN in Chicago,
as only be a few of the things for the winners.

The panel of judges were made up of well known radio, stage and screen
celebrities.

It was this contest that Buddy Swan won last year. Since winning the
contest he has made two pictures with Monogram namely, "The Ape" with
Boris Karloff and "Haunted House" and one RKO picture, "Citizen Kane".
He plays Orson Welles as a child.

MEMBER MUTUAL BROADCASTING SYSTEM

Chapter Ten

The whirlwind of activity began before the ink was dry. Press releases went out across the city and Bill Treadwell made announcements on the radio while the two winners introduced themselves to each other and made their way around the room to thank the judges and other contestants. There were contracts to sign, school arrangements to make, and proper wardrobes to be packed. The itinerary and publicity stops had all been preplanned, so the necessary preparations were kept to a minimum. The two preteen winners were stunned by their good fortune and secretly pinched themselves to be sure they weren't dreaming.

On Saturday, April 26, Colleen and Gary were introduced at a Palisades Park, New Jersey, beauty pageant and the winner of that contest accompanied the newly - crowned winners of the Uncle Don Talent Contest cross-country to California.

The chaperones and contest winners left for Hollywood on Sunday, May 4, 1941, stopping first in Chicago to visit Bridgeport native Edward Kelly the mayor of the "Windy City." Next stop, Mills Novelty Company, a business specializing in mechanical musical and the production of "soundies", three-minute musical 16 mm films featuring different genres of music shown in movie theaters between main attractions. The excited travelers were able to listen to many recordings and drink plenty of Coca-Cola, publicizing the newly introduced vending machines manufactured by the company.

From there they were off to the Oriental Theater to meet famed actor Bela Lugosi who was in costume ready to go on stage. After signing Colleen's cherished autograph book, and at the request of co-winner Gary Cole, the fanged thespian placed his signature on Colleen's slender neck. She remarked, "He's such a gentleman, even if he is Dracula."

The start of an exciting adventure!
Colleen Bartram, Gary Cole, and Uncle Don in WOR
Radio Station

TALENT KIDS

GUESTS OF MILLS NOVELTY

The two happiest kids in the country, Colleen Bartram and Gary Cole, Conn., winners of the Fourth Annual Uncle Don Talent Contest, sponsored by WOR, were visitors and guests at Mills Novelty Company last month. Colleen and Gary were selected from 3,000 entrants in the contest and their prize was a trip to Hollywood. Colleen, 10, won on her acrobatic dancing and Gary, 12, for his singing. They were escorted by Bill Treadwell, Uncle Don's assistant and a New York newspaperman.

Included in the party was lovely Myrtle Dietz, selected by the New York Optometrists as the best looking girl wearing glasses. Miss Dietz will be seen in the future in various optical advertising of the association.

Empress, Colleen Bartram and Gary Cole.

The party was received at noon by Mayor Edward Kelly and after lunch proceeded to Mills where they were welcomed by Ralph, Herb, Hayden Mills and Jim Mangan, advertising manager. The kids were thrilled by the Soundies and meeting Bert Mills, inventor of Panoram. They were also given a chance to drink all the Coca-Cola they wanted by Jack Walsh, manager of the beverage vender division at Mills. They saw ice cream made and drawn fresh from Mills freezer in the laboratory.

Another big thrill came when Herb Mills presented Gary and Colleen with RCA Midget Radios. Gary was delighted because it was going to give him an opportunity to listen to ball games all the way out to Hollywood and Colleen said it was

Myrtle Dietz, specs beauty, and Panoram.

15

sure something none of the other girls in Bridgeport had.

Leaving Mills the folks went on to the Oriental Theatre to meet Bela Lugosi. It was almost time for him to make his stage appearance as "Dracula," so the kids met him in all his horror glory. They decided he wasn't as bad as he's been painted though and got him to autograph a copy of Jim Mangan's "We're All Americans." The kids had sheet music with Kate Smith's picture on it. "Put your name around her neck," suggested Gary and Bela obliged. Colleen's comments about the film bogey man were—"He's such a gentleman, even if he is Dracula."

16

Bill Trau, Dolly Sarley and Jean Flynn at the Sicking showing of Panoram.

SOUNDIE MACHINE
TO AID RECRUITING

Now that the Army is being mechanized, recruiting for the armed forces of the United States also is being mechanized.

At 10 o'clock this morning the first mechanical Army recruiting device in the country will go into action in City Hall. In the lobby will be placed one of the new Soundie machines and in the machine will be a ten-minute Army film entitled The Air Army.

Capt. Winston V. Morrow, in charge of recruiting here, who received the film from recruiting headquarters at Syracuse Saturday, announced that the movie gives any person interested an excellent view of the Army Air Corps in peace and in wartime.

It shows airplanes flying in formation, pictures them operating in the field in cooperation with tanks and armored divisions, gives examples of dive bombing and its effects, shows the release of bombs, the courses of the missiles and the effect of the latter. The training of the recruit to become a pilot also is portrayed.

Capt. Morrow said the mechanical recruiting plan is being tried out here as a result of an idea conceived by Frank T. Curran, distributor in this area for Panoram Soundie machines. Curran donated the machine to be used today for the use of the Army.—*Buffalo, N. Y., Courier-Express.*

Colleen Bartram Is Test Winner

Ten-Year Old Dancer Will Be Tested for Movies In Hollywood

Colleen Bartram, ten year old daughter of Mr. and Mrs. Francis Bartram of 1729 Main St., is off to Hollywood on May 5th, for a series of screen tests. The little girl who took top honors in a field of more than 4,000 child performers, has studied acrobatic, toe, tap and tap-on-toe dancing at the Bessie Marie Reilly School of Stage Dancing for the past six years.

Next Wednesday evening Colleen will cut the tape and officially open the Palisades Park in New Jersey. That same evening, she will guest-star on Ben Bernie's program.

While in Hollywood, she will visit at Gene Autry's Ranch, meet Shirley Temple, and be entertained at tea by Jane Withers.

Colleen will be back in Bridgeport in time to appear in the annual recital of the Bessie Marie Reilly School of Dancing at the Mosque on Friday evening, May 23. At that time she will receive her sterling silver sixth year class pin.

A trip to the exhibit of Santa Fe Trains at the Chicago Museum rounded out the tour, then it was on to the Grand Canyon in Arizona, a much-prized destination for the Santa Fe Railroad.

Train Museum

The sprawling desert and huge ravines of the Grand Canyon were magnificent, especially to two young kids who had previously stayed close to home. A favorite spot to visit was the El Tovar Hotel, perched on a large flat mesa in New Mexico. Both locals and celebrities enjoyed the rustic exterior and cowboy décor. For two days, the children rode donkeys into the cavernous maw of the Grand Canyon, not knowing what lay ahead and never daring to look back as they followed switchbacks and curvy trails. They listened to braying donkeys clopping down the trails and held their breath when stones and pebbles tumbled down the canyon walls. Aware that their schoolmates were studying for exams and finishing up the final weeks of the school year, both were grateful for their new experiences. They greeted each morning with a sense of anticipation for whatever lay ahead. At night they ran each day's exciting events over and over in their minds as they lay down to sleep, wrapped in a blanket of awe and contentment.

El Tovar Hotel - Grand Canyon Arizona

Photo Courtesy of Common.Wikimedia.org

El Tovar Hotel

Photo Courtesy of Flickr.com

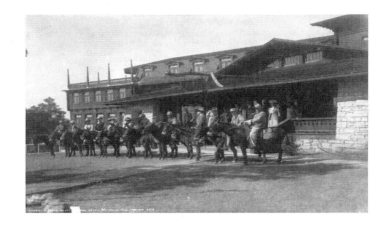

Photo courtesy of Pinterest.com

Chapter Eleven

The seventeen-hour train ride to Los Angeles was another adventure not to be forgotten. There wasn't much to see at night except occasional sparkles of scattered city lights against the dusky horizon, but during the day the southwestern landscape filled them with wonder. After dinner in the roomy dining car, the adults caught up on the latest gossip from high-profile Hollywood columnists Louella Parsons and Hedda Hopper and enjoyed cocktails while the children amused themselves with card games and questions about their upcoming tour of Hollywood. The publicity savvy adults coached Colleen and Gary on the importance of good posture, bright smiles, and appropriate diction as they prepared for their whirlwind tour of the "City of Angels."

The wheels clacked like a stopwatch ticking the miles away as passengers tried to slumber until everyone drifted off to sleep lulled by the gentle rocking of the sleeper berths.

Colleen and Gary fidgeted in their seats when the

train pulled into the city of Los Angeles. The conductor directed them to the nearest exits and smiled at the giggling children. The entourage was delighted at the sight of towering palm trees lining the streets like sentinels guarding the secrets of fame and fortune from tourists' curious eyes.

Through his many contacts in the advertising industry, Bill Treadwell had made arrangements for his troupe of East Coasters to stay at the renowned Biltmore Hotel. Not only would he benefit from the publicity associated with their stay, but the hotel's generous gesture towards WOR and its affiliates would be noted on both coasts.

The train to California that gives so much for so little!

The train's uniformed courier-nurse on the Scout gives mothers a helping hand with their babies and children, and assists all other passengers requesting her free and friendly service.

There's comfort and beauty in the Scout's glinting stainless steel chair cars, with their deeply cushioned adjustable seats, individual lights, broad windows, spacious dressing rooms!

The Santa Fe Scout

The Famous Santa Fe Economy Train That Makes it Easy and Pleasant to Save Travel-Dollars on Your California Trip

Let's talk Scout fares first. You can't obtain lower rail fares on any other transcontinental road or train!

● One-way fare, between Chicago and Los Angeles, San Diego, or San Francisco, in Scout chair cars (no berth required), $39.50; round-trip (over 60% miles) only 66%. One-way fare, in Scout sleeping cars, $49.50; round-trip fare, only $74. Berth charges extra.

Scout meals? They're delightful, generous, served by Fred Harvey. Seven regular meals on the Scout, between Chicago and Los Angeles, need cost you but $2.05! Special children's menus, too.

Scout patrons write constantly of their appreciation of the alert helpfulness of the Courier-Nurse; the friendly courtesy of the train crew; the cheery special car for women and children, and the air-conditioned comfort of this popular train.

The natural color photos shown here will tell you the story of the daily Scout like nothing else can—and enable you to

see for yourself why this fine, swift Santa Fe train can give you so much for so little on your transcontinental journey this summer.

Grand Canyon ● Yosemite Park Golden Gate Exposition

Santa Fe is the only railroad entering Grand Canyon National Park. So be sure to spend a day or so enjoying the indescribable grandeur of this year-round wonderland when you travel to or from California on the Scout.

Then, too, via Santa Fe, you can easily include in your western trip the sunny beaches of Southern California, Yosemite's majestic waterfalls, lakes, and big trees in the high Sierras; and San Francisco's beautiful Golden Gate Exposition, opening May 25th, 1940.

● If you buy a California round-trip ticket via Santa Fe both ways, from Chicago or other Eastern points, you may include San Diego, Los Angeles and San Francisco at no extra ticket cost!

Sleep tight, little man, in your snowy Scout bed, while the long miles slip smoothly away! In Scout sleeping cars, rail fares and berth charges are only about half those in standard Pullmans!

The Scout's modern lounge car, with its beautiful cocktail bar, is for the especial pleasure of sleeping car passengers.

And here's Santa Fe's famous day-saving dollar-saving streamliner

El Capitan

The West's only all-chair-car transcontinental streamliner

This gay economy stainless steel flyer, carrying ultra-modern chair cars, Fred Harvey diner, and lounge car, whisks between Chicago and Los Angeles in just 39¾ hours! One way fare, only $39.50, plus $5 extra fare; round-trip $66, plus $10 extra fare ● Mail coupon for free booklet.

T. B. Gallaher, P.T.M., Santa Fe System Lines 1160 Railway Exchange, Chicago, Illinois

Please send me free the new Scout booklet containing natural color photos; El Capitan Booklet; and fares from _____

_____ to _____

Name _____

Address _____

THE SCOUT

WESTBOUND	NO. 1	DAILY
Central Standard Time		
Lv. Chicago..........A. T. & S. F.	10.25 PM	Sun.
Ar. Kansas City	8.00 AM	Mon.
Lv. Kansas City " "	9.15 AM	
Lv. Newton	1.50 PM	
Lv. Wichita	2.45 PM	
Lv. Amarillo..........P. & S. F.	12.05 AM	Tues.
Ar. Clovis..........A. T. & S. F.	2.36 AM	
Mountain Standard Time		
Lv. Clovis..........A. T. & S. F.	1.55 AM	
Lv. Belen	8.45 AM	
Ar. Williams	5.53 AM	
Lv. Williams..........(Bus)	6.00 PM	Tues.
Ar. Grand Canyon	7.45 PM	
Lv. Grand Canyon..........(Bus)	4.00 PM	Tues.
Ar. Williams	5.45 PM	
Pacific Standard Time		
Lv. Williams..........A. T. & S. F.	5.53 PM	Tues.
Ar. Ash Fork	6.45 PM	
Ar. Barstow..........A. T. & S. F.	3.10 AM	Wed.
Ar. San Bernardino	5.45 AM	
Ar. Pasadena	8.00 AM	
Ar. Los Angeles	8.30 AM	
Lv. Los Angeles..........A. T. & S. F.	9.20 AM	
Ar. San Diego	12.45 PM	

Connecting Trains

	NO. 1	DAILY
Lv. Clovis..........A. T. & S. F.	3.00 AM	Tues.
Ar. Carlsbad	8.15 AM	
Lv. Carlsbad..........A. T. & S. F.	8.00 AM	Mon.
Ar. Clovis	1.25 AM	Tues.
Lv. Albuquerque..........A. T. & S. F.	6.00 AM	Tues.
Ar. Belen	6.50 AM	
Lv. Belen..........A. T. & S. F.	8.35 AM	Tues.
Ar. Albuquerque	9.25 AM	
Lv. Barstow..........A. T. & S. F.	7.45 AM	Wed.
Ar. Bakersfield	11.30 AM	
Ar. Oakland	7.50 PM	
Ar. San Francisco	8.15 PM	

EASTBOUND	NO. 2	DAILY
Pacific Standard Time		
Lv. San Diego..........A. T. & S. F.	4.15 PM	Sun.
Ar. Los Angeles	6.45 PM	
Lv. Los Angeles..........A. T. & S. F.	8.15 PM	Sun.
Lv. Pasadena	8.45 PM	"
Lv. San Bernardino " "	10.10 PM	
Lv. Barstow	12.40 AM	Mon.
Mountain Standard Time		
Lv. Ash Fork..........A. T. & S. F.	10.55 AM	
Ar. Williams	11.59 AM	
Lv. Williams..........(Bus)	6.00 PM	Mon.
Ar. Grand Canyon	7.45 PM	
Lv. Grand Canyon..........(Bus)	8.00 AM	Mon.
Ar. Williams	9.45 AM	
Lv. Williams..........A. T. & S. F.	11.59 AM	Mon.
Ar. Belen	8.10 PM	
Ar. Clovis	2.15 AM	Tues.
Central Standard Time		
Lv. Clovis..........A. T. & S. F.	3.30 AM	
Ar. Amarillo..........P. & S. F.	5.50 AM	
Ar. Wichita..........A. T. & S. F.	3.15 PM	
Ar. Newton	4.05 PM	
Ar. Kansas City	9.19 PM	
Ar. Kansas City	10.00 PM	
Ar. Chicago	8.45 AM	Wed.

Connecting Trains

	NO. 2	DAILY
Lv. San Francisco..........A. T. & S. F.	10.20 AM	Sun.
Lv. Oakland	10.45 AM	
Lv. Bakersfield " "	7.10 PM	
Ar. Barstow	10.55 PM	
Lv. Belen..........A. T. & S. F.	8.40 PM	Mon.
Ar. Albuquerque	9.30 PM	"
Lv. Albuquerque..........A. T. & S. F.	7.10 PM	Mon.
Ar. Belen	8.00 PM	"
Lv. Clovis..........A. T. & S. F.	3.00 AM	Tues.
Ar. Carlsbad	8.15 AM	
Lv. Carlsbad..........A. T. & S. F.	8.00 PM	Mon.
Ar. Clovis	1.25 AM	Tues.

(Schedule subject to change without notice)

Courtesy of Wikipedia

Chapter Twelve

Entering the Biltmore Hotel in Los Angeles was like being hugged by a gilded Grandma bedecked in ornate jewels. Her cathedral ceilings, sculpted walls, and highly polished floors wove an intricate pattern of opulence throughout each of the eleven floors. Delicate crystal chandeliers hung like fireflies frozen in flight and everything from hidden speakeasies to elaborate dining rooms graced the cavernous ballrooms and hallways. It may have reminded some of the visitors of the yellow brick road in the recently released *Wizard of Oz* movie starring Judy Garland.

Adhering to a strict schedule, Treadwell and his guests made their way to the RKO studio lot in Culver City. RKO Pictures, aka RKO Radio Pictures, had worked with many up and coming stars including Bette Davis, Cary Grant, and Bridgeport native Robert Mitchum. Their musicals showcased the talents of Fred Astaire and Ginger Rogers and animated films proved to be lucrative in theatres across the United States. Arrangements for "meet and greets" with other rising stars had been made prior to their arrival and the media used this opportunity to photograph and publicize every detail of the visits. Some of the early stars the duo met included:

Radio stars **Fibber McGee and Molly**

Wendy Barrie – *worked alongside Basil Rathbone in "Hounds of Baskerville" and Humphrey Bogart in "Dead End".*

Leon Errol – *worked with Lana Turner in "Dancing Co-Ed" and worked on "The Girl from Mexico".*

Ethel Barrymore – *known as "First Lady of the American Theater" for her many theater performances and starred with Lionel Barrymore in "Rasputin and the Empress".*

Brenda Joyce – *appeared in "Little Old New York" with Fred MacMurray and "The Rains Came" with Tyrone Power and Myrna Loy. She went on to star in several Tarzan movies.*

Adolphe Menjou – *appeared in "A Star is Born" with Janet Gaynor, and "Farewell to Arms" with Frederic March.*

George Sanders – *starred in "House of Seven Gables" and "The Saint Takes Over".*

Bob Sterling *– started his career in movies and went on to star in the TV series "Topper" as George Kirby along with Leo G. Carroll and Anne Jeffreys.*

Charlie Chan *– star of numerous movies followed by many fans.*

The trip provided a wealth of photo opportunities and helped endear the stars to their fans. Uncle Don benefited greatly when studio heads praised his contest winners and WOR gained sponsors as reports of the visit reached the airwaves. It was a 'win-win' once again. Stage mothers everywhere must have envied Murph Bartram and her talented daughter. Local papers reported on the wonderful event and Colleen was invited back to Hollywood once the school year was finished.

Biltmore Hotel Los Angeles CA

Courtesy of flickr.com

Courtesy of Millenium Biltmore Hotel

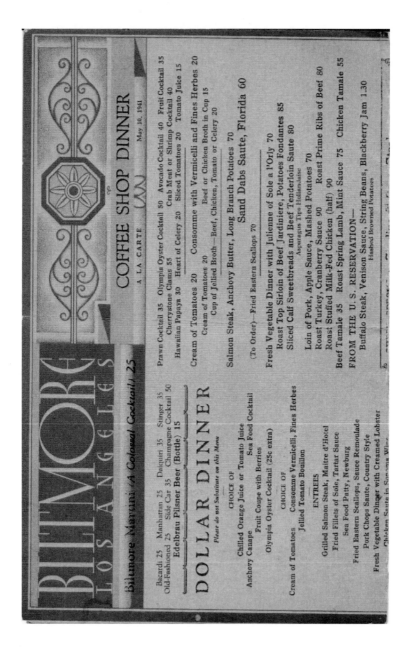

with French Fried Potatoes, New Peas 1.10

(GRAIN FED)

(From The Grill, To Order) — Spring Chicken (half) 90   Broiled Squab Chicken (half) 70
Steak Minute 1.00   Top Sirloin 80   Sirloin Steak 1.25   Tenderloin Steak 1.25
Lamb Chops (2) 80

Imp. Norwegian Sardines (box) 50   Assorted Meats 80   Spring Lamb 75
Imp. French or Portuguese Sardines (box) 70   Cold Prime Ribs of Beef 80
Sliced Ham 70   Home-Made Head Cheese, Potato Salad 50   Beef Tongue 65

Chef's Salad with Dark Meat of Chicken 60 — White Meat 80
Fruit Salad 40   Grapefruit Salad 45   Lettuce and Tomato 30   Celery and Apple 30
Stuffed Tomato with Chicken 45   Calavo Salad (or Half Shell) 40
Prawn, Shrimp or Crab Meat Salad 50   Tuna 35   Vegetable 50   Combination 35
Fresh Asparagus 40   Chicken 50   Chef's Salad with Prawns 75
Served with French or Mayonnaise Dressing   Roquefort Dressing 15   Thousand Island 10

Fried Eggplant 20   New Peas 25   Creamed Spinach 20   Succotash 25
Corn Saute with Green Peppers 30   Golden Bantam Corn on Cob 20
Banana Squash 25   New String Beans 25   Mashed Turnips 20
Fresh Asparagus 40   Broccoli Hollandaise 40   Artichoke, Drawn Butter 30

Mashed Potatoes 15   Boiled Potatoes 10   French Fried 15   Baked Potatoes 20

Jack Cheese 15   Philadelphia Cream 20   American 20   Cottage 20   Imp. Swiss 25

Cup of Coffee 10   Pot of Coffee 15   Pot of Tea 15   Iced Tea or Coffee 10   Buttermilk 10
Certified Guernsey Milk, Small Bottle 10 — Large 15   Homogenized Milk, Large 15
If you use Saccharine instead of Sugar, we have it! Ask the waitress

Liberty Cream Pie 20   Fresh Strawberry Cake 35
Green Apple Pie 15   Pumpkin Pie 15   French Pastry 15   Assorted Cakes 20
Old-Fashioned Strawberry Shortcake 30
Fresh Strawberries or Youngberries and Cream 30
Imperial Cantaloupe 35   Fresh Raspberries 35

CUSTARDS — Coffee, Chocolate or Vanilla 20   Caramel Custard 25   Rice Pudding 20
ICES — Orange, Raspberry, Lemon or Pineapple 15
ICE CREAM — Almond Roca, Strawberry, Vanilla, Chocolate, Peppermint or Coffee 20

Plus 3% Sales Tax   *The COFFEE SHOP is under the supervision of MISS ROSE ENGLE*

Calf Liver Saute with Bacon
Breaded Pork Cutlet, Cream Sauce
Roast Spring Lamb, Mint Sauce
Roast Stuffed Tom Turkey, Cranberry Sauce
Roast Leg of Pork, Apple Butter
Prime Ribs of Grain-Fed Beef au Jus
(COLD) — Assorted Cold Meats, Home-Made Headcheese
Prime Ribs of Beef, Chef's Salad
Sliced Leg of Lamb, Beet Salad

25c Extra (*Cooked to Order*)
Idaho Brook Trout (Saute or Broiled)
Spring Chicken Saute, Country Style, Apple Butter
Minute Steak Saute, Sauce Bercy
Broiled Lamb Chops with Bacon

50c Extra (*Cooked to Order*)
Broiled Sirloin Steak, Maitre d'Hotel
Roast Stuffed Squab en Casserole with Peas

New String Beans Fleurette   Hashed in Cream Potatoes
Baby Carrots
(Large Baked Potato 10c extra)

CHOICE OF
Romaine and Tomatoes, French Dressing

Liberty Cream Pie   Old-Fashioned Strawberry Shortcake
Pumpkin Pie   Rice Pudding   Vanilla Custard   Pound Cake
Grapenut Ice Cream Roll, Vanilla Sauce   Biscuit Tortoni
ICE CREAM: Coffee, Chocolate, Almond Roca, Vanilla,
Strawberry or Peppermint
SHERBETS: Raspberry, Pineapple, Orange or Lemon
SPECIAL: Baronet or Golden Rich Cheese
American, Domestic Swiss or Jack Cheese and Crackers
Coffee   Tea   Milk

JOHN COLL, *Maitre D'Hotel*

Fibber McGee and Molly with Colleen Bartram and Gary Cole

Hollywood CA. Courtesy of RKO Pictures © 1941

Colleen Bartram, Wendy Barrie, and Gary Cole.

Hollywood CA. Courtesy of RKO Pictures © 1941

Colleen Bartram, Leon Errol, and Gary Cole

Hollywood CA. Courtesy of RKO Pictures © 1941

*Gary Cole, Ethel Barrymore, Colleen Bartram, and
Uncle Don*

Hollywood CA. Courtesy of RKO Pictures © 1941

COLLEEN BARTRAM, E. Main St. singing and dancing wonder, who bested thousands of kids in a nation-wide contest, is shown above with the Queen of the Royal Barrymore family, Ethel.

An audience with stage queen and a trip to Hollywood for a screen test comprised Colleen's reward.

*Bill Treadwell, Gary Cole, Brenda Joyce, Colleen Bartram
and Myrtle Joyce*

Hollywood CA. Courtesy of RKO Pictures © 1941

*Colleen Bartram, Adolphe Menjou (signing Colleen's
autograph book), and Gary Cole.*

Hollywood CA. Courtesy of RKO Pictures © 1941

Gary Cole, Colleen Bartram, and George Sanders

Hollywood CA. Courtesy of RKO Pictures © 1941

*Bill Treadwell, Colleen Bartram, Bob Sterling (signing
Colleen's autograph book),
Gary Cole, and Myrtle Dietz
Hollywood CA. Courtesy of RKO Pictures © 1941*

Myrtle Dietz, Gary Cole, Charlie Chan, Colleen Bartram, Corbina Wright, and Bill Treadwell. Hollywood CA. Courtesy of RKO Pictures © 1941

Personal scrapbook of Colleen Bartram varied sources.

Colleen Joan Bartram Returns to Dance Here

Colleen Joan Bartram returned yesterday from Hollywood to take part in the annual dance recital which the pupils of Bessie Marie Reilly will present Friday evening in the Pyramid Mosque.

A pupil at the Reilly school for the last six years, Colleen last month won a talent contest conducted by Station WOR and was sent to Hollywood for screen tests. She will return to Hollywood next month.

Local newspaper 1941

Chapter Thirteen

On the surface the offer to return to Hollywood seemed like a dream come true for any youngster wishing to pursue a career in entertainment, however, the reality of working in an ever-changing industry wasn't as glamorous as many people believed. Hollywood was undergoing growing pains. Technological inroads were being made; the creative aspects of the industry were changing, and seeds of dissention were growing as America headed into World War II.

The motion picture industry had significant impact on how current events were perceived not only in America, but in the world. Different perspectives caused studios to teeter on the edge and many turned to producing propaganda films for support of the war effort. Conversely, they also portrayed fictional characters engaged in unpatriotic behaviors paving the way for accusations of communism and blacklisting in the near future.

Gangster tales, film noir, and musicals still appealed to the masses, but an undercurrent of paranoia tinged productions coming out of certain studios. Short films touched on political themes and feature films like Warner Bros. *Confessions of a Nazi Spy,* a tale about a Nazi spy ring led by nefarious leader Franz Schlager (George Sanders) foiled by patriotic FBI agent Edward Renard (Edward G. Robinson) realistically tackled the perceived threat of Nazism. Charlie Chaplin's film *The Great Dictator* addressed Hitler's rise to power and, shortly thereafter, *Yankee Doodle Dandy* starring James Cagney ushered in another rousing round of patriotism.

Paranoia and uncertainty fueled fears of subliminal pro-communistic ideals in movies dealing with Russia. *Mission to Moscow*, originally intended to foster good will between the US and Soviet Union, came under scrutiny for its positive portrayal of life in Russia. Critics feared the film glorified the leaders of a communist nation and advised viewers not to see it. Walt Disney and Ronald Reagan cautioned the entertainment industry to be vigilant in detecting any pro-communistic tendencies within Hollywood circles and an underlying fear of infiltration by dissidents affected movie goers and movie makers across the USA.

Frank and Murph were avid fans of movies and watched the meteoric rise of Shirley Temple beginning in 1935, noting her waning popularity as she grew older. Gossip columnists documented the emerging child-actor phenomena and took note when ambitious studio heads changed the names of many young actors and actresses including Judy Garland (real name Frances Ethel Gumm), Mickey

Rooney (real name Joe Yule Jr.), and Bobby/Robert Blake (Mickey Gubitosi), for example. Stars were groomed to fit an image carefully crafted by their respective studio heads and were often subjected to harsh working conditions. Frank and Murph didn't want their young daughter manipulated by callous businessmen thousands of miles from home which was one of many factors that led to their decision to decline the invitation offered to them to return to the Golden State.

On a more personal note, Murph did not want to uproot her family for an uncertain future 3,000 miles away. It was hard enough feeding and clothing kids in Connecticut, but at least she had family throughout the area. Moving at any time was difficult, and she felt that to do so during war was foolhardy. Better to stay put and continue along the path they had cleared than to go into the unknown with no guide. Murph had plans for her daughter, and Colleen wanted to stay in school and concentrate on her goal of attending business college.

Back home in Bridgeport, Colleen continued to perform at the Bessie Marie Reilly School of Stage Dancing and other venues while maintaining a casual business relationship with WOR and Uncle Don. For his part, Don turned to selling war bonds. He and his publicist Bill Treadwell sent letters to Colleen and Murph asking them to appear on stage at certain locations to sell bonds, capitalizing on Colleen's fame as a WOR Contest Winner. As soon as one appearance was finished, another was booked and Colleen scurried all over town at Uncle Don's behest. Murph finally decided the constant running back and forth interfered with Colleen's school and dance studies and told Don they would no longer participate, feeling they had done their fair share in the war effort.

For her part, Colleen was relieved not to rush home from school, change into her costume, endure Murph's pulling and yanking, as they prepared for yet another patriotic rally. She continued to practice her dance routines, read her favorite books, and caught up on family news and her siblings activities. There were no cozy mother-daughter teas or outings. Murph kept strict control over any and all of her daughter's activities both in and out of home.

In 1942 Colleen received a special Seventh year certificate from the Bessie Marie Reilly School of Stage Dancing. She was only 11 years old and had already crossed the United States as a professional performer.

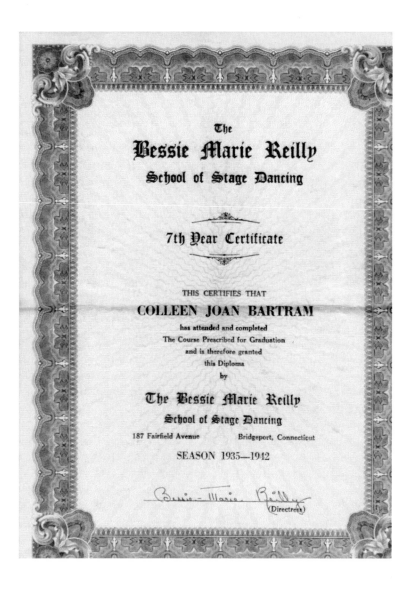

The

Bessie Marie Reilly
School of Stage Dancing

7th Year Certificate

THIS CERTIFIES THAT

COLLEEN JOAN BARTRAM

has attended and completed
The Course Prescribed for Graduation
and is therefore granted
this Diploma
by

The Bessie Marie Reilly
School of Stage Dancing

187 Fairfield Avenue   Bridgeport, Connecticut

SEASON 1935—1942

(Directress)

THIS IS YOUR Ten-Cent *Defense* Stamp Album. Fill it with 187 Ten-Cent Defense Stamps. Add 5c in coin, and it will have a value of $18.75. Exchange it at the post office for a Defense Savings Bond which, after 10 years, will be worth $25. Then start filling another Defense Stamp Album.

Defense Stamps are sold in five denominations—10c, 25c, 50c, $1, and $5. With your first purchase of any Defense Stamp, you are entitled to receive, free of charge, an Album for mounting that kind of Stamp.

Mount none but 10c Defense Stamps in this Album. Be sure to affix Stamps securely.

AS YOU FILL this Album with Defense Stamps it will rapidly grow in value and should be guarded against theft or loss. A precaution is to carry your Album in a self-addressed stamped envelope, with a written request on the envelope to return to you if found.

This Album is the property of—

Name . . . .

Address . . . .

City . . . . State . . . .

10c	20c	30c	40c	50c	60c	70c
80c	90c	$1.00	$1.10	$1.20	$1.30	$1.40
$1.50	$1.60	$1.70	$1.80	$1.90	$2.00	$2.10

Courtesy of pinterest.com

Chapter Fourteen

O ver the next few years the world plunged into war. Rosie the Riveter was featured prominently on posters, and women literally rolled up their sleeves and pitched in to help the war effort, replacing men in factories, freeing them to fight. Sisters and daughters stayed home and resourceful families pooled their resources to provide for their families. Murph took a job in a local factory while family members cared for her children.

Teenage son Francis Jr. had watched his little sister hone her skills and talent with a mixture of jealousy, awe, and hidden pride. As she continued her work as a performer and headliner across the city of Bridgeport, he decided to attend the prestigious Fairfield Preparatory School, an all-male Catholic Jesuit school located in Fairfield, CT. To afford the steep tuition of over $1000 per school year (equivalent to approximately $13,000 in 2017), Murph switched Colleen from a private Catholic school to Warren Harding High, a public school in

Bridgeport.

Colleen enjoyed the less restrictive and informal atmosphere of a public high school vs. the strict regimens of Catholic school. She continued to dance and perform occasionally taking the train to nearby New York City where entertainment and opportunities to perform were an integral part of the city's creative core.

Frank and Murph continued to work, seeing each other at mealtime to catch up on the events of the day and review their strict budget. The children pitched in with household chores and on many nights Colleen prepared for performances late into the night. One notable performance was on May 25, 1946, Colleen's sixteenth birthday. Not only did she dance, but younger sister Audrey shared billing as a dancer in a skit.

Colleen was apprehensive about the routine knowing Audrey's penchant for mischievousness. She coached her little sister as best she could and encouraged her to behave during rehearsal. Colleen knew all too well that Murph would be tracking their every move from the wings of the auditorium. She hugged Audrey before the performance, whispered a few encouraging words into her ear, and the show went off without a hitch. The family enjoyed Wacky Chocolate Cake to celebrate her birthday that night.

Overshadowing her Sweet Sixteen birthday celebration was the announcement by her older brother that he would be attending the revered and expensive Holy Cross College in Worcester, MA., an all-male Catholic Jesuit school where he enrolled in a

specialty program called Naval Reserve Officers
Training Corps or NROTC, planning to become a
Navy officer. The annual costs were steep-
approximately $1200-$1300 per year (approximate
value today $17,000). While some students qualified
for financial assistance in the NROTC program,
those monies were limited to tuition and books and
did not cover other fees. Considering the annual
household budget for the Bartrams was roughly
$3600, the cost to send young Francis to college
would be nearly one-half of that amount. Murph
wasn't concerned with the cost – her daughter would
graduate soon and she'd contribute to her big
brother's college fees.

On June 21, 1947, the senior class of Warren
Harding High School in Bridgeport donned their
caps and gowns, each student hoping for success in a
variety of fields and professions. Among the class of
515 graduating students, Colleen Bartram stood out
amongst her peers as a shining example of success
and perseverance. Since the age of five, she had
honed her athletic skills and learned new dance
moves. She had taken a College Preparatory
Curriculum in high school, but her mother had other
plans for her.

Colleen already knew where and what she would
be doing – Murph had made sure of that. On
Monday, June 23, her autograph book tucked inside
her purse, her suitcase firmly clutched in her hands,
the new graduate boarded a train for New York City
and took a window seat for the nearly two-hour ride
and reported for work at the Roxy Theatre. By

Monday night she was a high-kicking part of the dancing ensemble called the Roxyettes, the forerunner of Radio City Music Hall's famed Rockettes.

IF YOU ARE INTERESTED IN BEING CONSIDERED FOR OUR
FAIR TOURING LINES

PLEASE REPORT TO ROXY THEATRE BACKSTAGE

West 51st Street near 7th Ave.

MONDAY JUNE 9, 1947 at 11 A. M.

BRING TAP SHOES AND SHORT REHEARSAL CLOTHES.

Lucy Baldino
1297 _____ Street
"Ever stretching forth a willing hand of service."
National Honor Society 4; Scholarship Leadership 3, 4; Ushers' Guild 3, 4; Vice-President of Class; _____ 3, 4; Dramatic Club 2; Spectator Editorial Board 4.

Anne Balogach
_____ Arctic Street
"I my duty to love them all."
Girls' Student League 2, 3, 4; Red Cross 2, 3, 4; Spectator Distribution staff 3, 4; Choir 2; Girls' Glee Club 4; Biology Club 3, 4; Spanish Club 3, 4.

Irene Balogach
38 Hallett Street
"Cheerful, modest and friendly, loving all, liked by all."
National Honor Society 4; Scholarship Leadership 3, 4; Ushers' Guild 3, 4; Athletic Association 3; War Stamps Representative 3; Spectator Editorial Board; Girls' Letter Club 3.

Robert Balogh
811 Pearl Harbor Street
"Whatever his hand findeth to do, it doth well."
Boys' Student League 2, 3, 4; Red Cross 2, 3; Corridor Guide 4.

Mary E. Bannon
Bldg. 43, Apt. 271, Success Park
"All my soul acts are deep, And I'm not feeling well."
Ushers' Guild 3, 4; President; Girls' Student League 2, 3, 4; Red Cross 3, 4; Biology Club 4; Corridor Guide 4.

Geraldine S. Barba
85 Howe Street
"Observes all—observed by all."
Girls' Student League 2, 3, 4; Red Cross 2, 3, 4; Choir 3, 4; Girls' Glee Club 2; Italian Club 2, 3.

Philip Baroff
385 North Bishop Avenue
"His heart belongs to sports."
Boys' Student League 2, 3, 4; Red Cross 3, 4; Athletic Association 3, 4; Football 4; Basketball 4; Baseball 3, 4.

Joan Barlow
296 Connecticut Avenue
"Her humorous ladyship."
Girls' Student League 2, 3, 4; Red Cross 2, 3, 4; Salvage Representative 3; Biology Club 2, 3, 4; Junior Traffic Club 2.

Colleen Bartram
50 Glen Place
*"She will dance her way to fame,
In bright lights you'll see her name."*
Girls' Student League 2, 3, 4; Red Cross 2, 3, 4; Cercle Francais 3, 4; Vice-President 4; Petit Cercle 2; Dramatic Club 3; Letter Club 3, 4.

Frances Marie Betsavage
_____ Logan Street
"Whatever mother makes, loyal friend."
Girls' Student League 2, 3, 4; Red Cross 3, 4; Home Room Leader 2; Salvage Representative 2.

Antoinette Battista
Apt. 306, Bldg. 43, Yellow Mill Village
"In her cheek there was a dimple."
Girls' Student League 2, 3, 4; Red Cross 3, 4; Senior Follies Staff 4; Choir 3, 4; Girls' Glee Club 3; Future Business Leaders 4; Secretarial Club 2.

Dorothy Baxter
_____ Stratford Street
"Her reddish hair relieves plain looks."
Girls' Student League 2, 3, 4; Red Cross 2, 3, 4; Salvage Representative 3, 4.

13

Colleen Bartram
High School photo 1947

Chapter Fifteen

I n order to perform in live stage performances, entertainers had to join the American Guild of Variety Artists (AGVA), a labor union with ties to the AFL-CIO. Founded in 1939 the AGVA worked on behalf of the scores of men and women in a variety of fields. According to their website (www.agva.use.com) the organization covered many aspects and details in performers' careers: *"...negotiates, sets and enforces salary minimums...conditions of employment such as rehearsal and performance hours, overtime provisions, safe and sanitary work conditions, travel stipulations, vacation and sick pay, publicity and promotion, audition procedures and general work rules."* Dues were based on income earned during the prior months and varied from person to person.

Colleen joined AGVA and diligently reported her income and paid her dues. She worked long hours, rehearsed alone and with precision dancers, choreographing each move and each step to reduce the likelihood of injury and still entertain. Residents of Bridgeport were proud of their child-star turned

New York City performer and continued to track her
adventures as a glamorous Roxyette.

The ensemble of young women danced in New
York City and out-of-town locations that
necessitated bus or train trips. They packed their
costumes and make-up in suitcases, small trunks, and
hat boxes and rolled merrily down the highway.
Rehearsals were frequent. Show times were posted
on doors and each young lady did their best to share
their limited accommodations with others, including
the coveted powder room. They entertained
audiences with choreographed moves and bowed
gracefully to a thundering applause at the end of the
shows.

Every week Colleen dutifully sent Murph her
paycheck, keeping track of her earnings so she could
pay her AGVA dues when the time came. Her living
expenses included transportation back and forth
from New York to Bridgeport when her schedule
allowed along with expenditures for new costumes,
shoes, and makeup. Back at home, Francis Jr.
enjoyed college and didn't worry about tuition – his
hard-working sister footed the bill. Little sister
Audrey attended Sacred Heart Academy in Hamden,
CT., overcoming nagging health issues and
eventually graduating a year later than scheduled.

For two years Bridgeport's Sweetheart performed
in New York City with the all-girl Roxyette Revue.
Each night after massaging her tired feet with lotion,
she would carefully drape her dance clothes over a
chair to air them out, roll her auburn tresses into
tight pin curls and skewer them into place with

rubber-tipped bobby pins. Murph no longer waited in the wings ready to pounce and criticize. Dancing became less of a chore and more fun.

Roxy Theatre New York

Photo courtesy of flickr.com

Colleen Bartram (bottom row L to R second to last)
Roxyettes circa 1948

Colleen Bartram as Roxyette
second row L to R third person

Colleen Bartram on left

Photo courtesy of Weiss Photo

Colleen Bartram 1ˢᵗ on left

Courtesy of Weiss Photo

Colleen Bartram 1ˢᵗ on bottom row left

Paying Her Dues
*Note Designation: **Chorus***
Subject to change depending on job

Chapter Sixteen

By 1947 the United States had shifted from a war mentality to a national focus of peace and prosperity. NATO (the North Atlantic Treaty Organization) was established to strengthen the relationships between the U.S. and European allies and to act as a buffer to the Soviet Union's Warsaw Pact. The average wage was 70 cents an hour and television was fast becoming a favored form of entertainment. Polaroid sold its first camera for $89.95; movie theatres were filled with star-struck ladies watching crooner Frank Sinatra and hoofer Gene Kelly sing and dance their way across New York in "On the Town" while Rodgers and Hammerstein's production of "South Pacific" charmed audiences with the lyrical beckoning of Bali Ha'i and other enchanting songs.

One audience member watching the silver screen was a hard-working theatrical producer and former dancer named Billy Creedon. Born in Connecticut, he had the advantage of being close to Broadway and attended live performances regularly, whether in

New York or across the United States. Billy had a knack for spotting talented dancers who entertained with panache.

One group that caught his eye was The Fives Ames Sisters, siblings who danced and tumbled as acrobats. Originally from Boston, the Ames family settled in New York performing in the many theatres that filled busy streets. According to Brian Murphy on *Flickr*, Creedon was an agent for Mary Eloise Ames. and recruited her for a group called "The Three Wells" who performed on several USO tours. Afterwards Mary joined another acrobatic dance team called "The Three Rays", one of Creedon's many creations. When Mary Eloise left to get married at the end of WWII, Billy had to find replacements for his lineup of stage performers.

In late 1948, while on a talent hunt, Creedon noted the radiant beauty and graceful moves of eighteen-year-old Colleen Bartram. Creedon was familiar with her work ethic and skills since her name had appeared in newspapers throughout New York and Connecticut. He watched her tap dance and twirl on stage, never missing a step. He approached theatre manager Matt Saunders who was in charge of the group, and offered Colleen a position in the new international "Three Rays", a trio of women showcasing their athletic and comedic skills in what would be billed as "knockabout comedy".

Irish Eyes Are Smiling!— Rapidly getting to the top in vaudeville is Bridgeport's Colleen Bertram, protege of Matt Saunders. The perty dancer after two years in the Roxy, is one of the "Three Rays" International act, a "show-stopper."

Chapter Seventeen

Judy Alwaise, Gloria Maeli, and Colleen Bartram signed contracts with Billy Creedon and formed strong bonds as The Three Rays. Judy was from New York, Gloria hailed from New Jersey, and the trio represented the tristate area of the region. Their comedy and dance routines were strenuous and required trust and faith in each other's abilities. They practiced their individual skills and honed with utmost precision as they tumbled and whirled on stage. Knockabout comedy was a combination of pratfalls and slapstick requiring a thorough knowledge of body mechanics, a high level of athleticism, and exquisite timing. Minute details such as jumping, footwork, and tumbling played a crucial part in each carefully choreographed act.

The three young women were familiar with the inner workings of stage productions and preparation. They'd traveled frequently, especially Colleen who had ventured to Hollywood as a preteen. Each performer knew firsthand how and what to expect from "life on the road".

At first their bookings were scattered, but in late

spring their calendar filled up with gigs across New England. Theaters, nightclubs, VA hospitals, state fairs, and private appearances jockeyed for time on their calendar and trips became hectic for the trio. They worked holidays, birthdays, and other special dates, often missing family celebrations and keeping in touch with loved ones via telegram or brief long distance calls. Manager Billy Creedon booked as many dates as he could, some lasting for months. The girls kept up with the pace and learned to improvise and survive in cramped quarters. They paid their AGVA dues, important as membership ensured some semblance of safety while performing on the road. Colleen continued to dutifully send Murph a large percentage of her pay which financed her brother's hefty college tuition.

Because of the nature of the acts it was crucial the girls wore proper footwear, costumes, and makeup. Regular expenses included special acrobat shoes (averaging $7.00 per pair) which were often replaced every few months; boots were $40.00 annually, costume cleaning and maintenance approximately $60.00 a year, and makeup costs ran upwards of $160.00 per year. This included pancake, greasepaint, and specialized leg makeup.

The girls adapted to life on the road and traveled by train, bus, or automobile. Stays in certain locales were easier than others. They learned to hand wash costumes and other personal items which they hung in their bathrooms where steam from their showers took wrinkles and they shared toiletries and food when they could while mending costumes with needle and thread as they moved from place to place and hotel to hotel across the upper United States and into Canada.

Paychecks were divided into thirds, each young lady receiving the equivalent of nearly $11.00 per performance (by today's standards about $108.00). The rate of pay barely increased between 1949 – 1952 putting a strain on their budgets and delaying the payment of monthly expenses. There were no emergency funds or loans to be had; they were separate entities when it came to personal finances and expenditures.

The hours were long and some performances started close to midnight, making long days longer. It was hard to wind down after late night performances, but the camaraderie within the show biz community was strong. Acts often gathered in restaurants or bars to drink, eat and share stories while the world slept.

The tour routes crisscrossed and overlapped many times during 1949, 1950, and late into 1951. From Quebec to Kentucky to New York and up to Montreal, the dates and times cascaded one into another making it difficult to return home for visits.

Coleen One of The Three Rays

Colleen Bartram, daughter of Mr. and Mrs. Francis Bartram of 59 Glen place, turned down a Hollywood offer when she was winner of an Uncle Don radio contest a few years ago. She wanted to finish her schooling first—which she has done. Now, after two years as a dancer at the Roxy in New York, she has become a member of "The Three Rays", an international act which recently played the Palace theater in New York. The act has been booked for an appearance on Jack Haley's NBC television show March 15 at 9 p.m. In the photo, Colleen is the girl in the middle. Judy Alwaise is on the left; Gloria Maeli, right.

Judy, Colleen, and Grace – The Three Rays

Three RAYS

Personal Management
BILLY CREEDON

Personal Management
BILLY CREEDON

Clowning around

COLLEEN J. PALLAMARY

138

Knockabout Comedy

Hanging Out

Make-up and wardrobe -Judy, Grace, and Colleen

Fun at the beach

Sharing the bill with fellow Bridgeport native Robert Mitchum!

Pyramid in the sand

Having fun

Helping the Military War Effort

The Three Rays bottom right corner

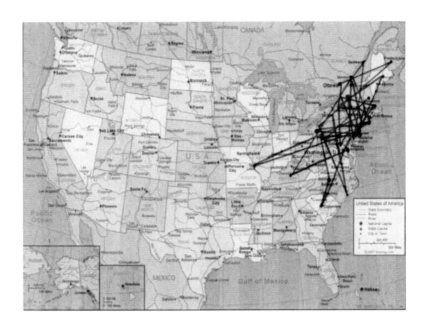

Tour Routes for The Three Rays 1949-1951

Calendar for Year 1949 (United States)

Calendar generated on www.timeanddate.com/calendar

Tour dates for 1949

Colleen's earnings approximately $2247

Average annual income $2950

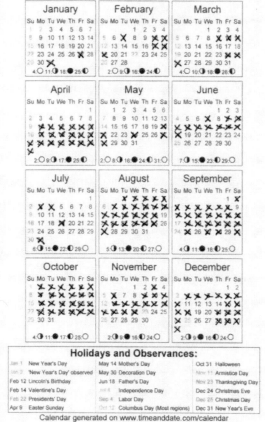

Tour dates for 1950

Colleen's earning approximately $1825

Average annual income $3210

Calendar for Year 1951 (United States)

January	February	March
Su Mo Tu We Th Fr Sa	Su Mo Tu We Th Fr Sa	Su Mo Tu We Th Fr Sa
X X X X X	1 2 3	1 X 3
7 8 X X X X X	4 5 X 7 8 9 10	4 5 6 7 8 9 10
X X X X X X X	11 12 13 14 15 16 17	11 12 13 14 X 16 17
X 22 23 24 25 X 27	18 19 20 21 22 23 24	18 19 20 21 22 23 24
X 29 30 31	25 26 27 28	25 26 X 28 29 30 31
1 ☽ 7 ● 14 ☾ 22 ○ 30 ☽	6 ● 13 ☾ 21 ○ 28 ☽	7 ● 15 ☾ 23 ○ 30 ☽

April	May	June
Su Mo Tu We Th Fr Sa	Su Mo Tu We Th Fr Sa	Su Mo Tu We Th Fr Sa
1 2 3 4 5 6 7	X X X X 5	1 2
X 9 10 11 X X X	X X X X X X X	3 4 5 6 7 8 9
X X X X X X X	X 14 15 16 17 X X	10 11 12 13 14 15 16
X X X X 26 27 28	20 21 22 23 24 25 26	17 18 19 20 21 22 23
29 X	27 28 29 30 31	24 25 26 27 28 29 30
6 ● 14 ☾ 21 ○ 28 ☽	5 ● 14 ☾ 21 ○ 27 ☽	4 ● 12 ☾ 19 ○ 26 ☽

July	August	September
Su Mo Tu We Th Fr Sa	Su Mo Tu We Th Fr Sa	Su Mo Tu We Th Fr Sa
1 2 3 4 5 6 7	1 2 3 4	1
8 9 10 11 12 13 14	X X X X X X	2 X X X X X X
X X X X X X X	X X X X X X X	9 10 X X X X X
X X X X X X X	X X X X X	16 17 X X X X X
29 30 31	26 X X X X X	23 X X X X X X
		30
4 ● 12 ☾ 18 ○ 25 ☽	2 ● 10 ☾ 16 ○ 24 ☽	1 ● 8 ☾ 15 ○ 23 ☽ 30 ●

October	November	December
Su Mo Tu We Th Fr Sa	Su Mo Tu We Th Fr Sa	Su Mo Tu We Th Fr Sa
1 2 3 4 5 6	1 2 3	X
7 8 9 10 11 12 13	4 5 6 7 8 X X	X X X X X X X
14 X X X X X X	X X X X X X X	X 10 11 12 13 14 15
21 22 23 24 25 26 27	X X X 28 29 X	16 17 18 X X X X
X 29 X 31	Y X X 28 29 X	X X X X X X X
		X X
7 ☾ 14 ○ 22 ☽ 30 ●	6 ☾ 13 ○ 21 ☽ 28 ●	5 ☾ 13 ○ 21 ☽ 28 ●

Holidays and Observances:

Jan 1 New Year's Day	May 13 Mother's Day	Oct 12 Columbus Day (Most regions)	Dec 25 Christmas Day
Feb 12 Lincoln's Birthday	May 30 Decoration Day	Oct 31 Halloween	Dec 31 New Year's Eve
Feb 14 Valentine's Day	Jun 17 Father's Day	Nov 11 Armistice Day	
Feb 22 Presidents' Day	Jul 4 Independence Day	Nov 22 Thanksgiving Day	
Mar 25 Easter Sunday	Sep 3 Labor Day	Dec 24 Christmas Eve	

Calendar generated on www.timeanddate.com/calendar

Tour dates for 1951

Colleen's earning approximately $1995

Average annual income $3510

***South America beginning November 9 ***

Chapter Eighteen

As a new decade dawned in a nation filled with fear, hope, and rejuvenation depending on where one focused. The Soviet Union exploded their first A-bomb in 1949, and fear of atomic warfare ran deep, as did the growth of Communism within certain parts of the world. Senator Joseph McCarthy used this time of fear as a catalyst for his attacks against Hollywood's writers, producers, and actors. A routine question to scores of people was "Are you now, or have you ever been, a member of the Communist Party?" Undaunted, Hollywood studios continued to release popular sci-fi, musical, and wartime films much to the delight of movie goers everywhere.

While the creative forces behind Hollywood productions were being questioned, the television industry was fast becoming a major contender for audiences. Westerns and comedies dominated the small screen and viewers eagerly awaited the "Hi Ho Silver" cry of Clayton Moore in *The Lone Ranger* or the marital mishaps and adventures of everyone's favorite Lucille Ball in *I Love Lucy*.

In addition to scripted formats and serialized stories, variety shows became a modernized extension of vaudeville featuring live performers. In the beginning stages of television programming, variety shows were not taped. Experienced entertainers understood the nuances and immediacy of live productions and used these to their advantage during television appearances. Sponsors and advertisers benefited from an increase in viewership and performers enjoyed the additional publicity and exposure television offered.

As a producer, manager, and astute businessman, Billy Creedon intuitively knew the tremendous value television offered. He booked the Three Rays on two variety programs. The Jack Haley Show, aka the Ford Star Revue, featured The Three Rays in March of 1951 on NBC. The very popular Texaco Star Theatre, hosted by funnyman Milton Berle, aka "Uncle Milty", welcomed The Three Rays in October of 1951. Television's popularity was skyrocketing and The Three Rays were along for the ride.

Creedon also took note of the fact that Latin America had become a beneficiary of sorts in its dealings with the US entertainment industry. In his book, *HOLLYWOOD A Very Short Introduction (Oxford University Press)*, author Peter Decherney notes that during World War II, Hollywood exported many films to Latin American countries in an effort to maintain cordial relations and to foster anti-communistic sentiments. Part of the cultural and conceptual exchange of creative efforts included live performances of musicians, acrobats, and others eager to share their talents with their neighbors down south. Creedon, in collaboration with producer Noel Sherman, booked The Three Rays and others for a Latin American tour called "Water Capers".

On November 4, 1951, Colleen, Judy, Grace, along with 47 other passengers, boarded Pan Am Flight AC 6694/04 at Idlewild Airport in New York (now JFK International), bound for Bogota, Colombia. One member of their entourage was a young Navy veteran named Michael J. Pallamary Jr., who had served on the battleship USS California and was now a drummer in the entertainment industry. Pallamary, recently divorced from his wife Regina, longed for an overseas adventure.

Photos courtesy of pinterest.com

Jack Haley aka The Scarecrow in the Wizard of Oz

TV *happiness shared by all the family!*

Model TF Pr—in mahogany and limed oak, 17-inch TV ... FM and AM radio ... 3-speed phonograph

Whether it's a party for friends or just a quiet evening at home ... your Motorola TV will add plenty of pleasure with its variety of entertainment. Drama, music, sports and educational programs ... all these are yours on Motorola's big-screen, phone-perfect television! Hear your favorite recorded music faithfully reproduced with Motorola's dependable and easy-to-operate "Multi-Play" record changer. And for the best in both FM and AM radio, there is nothing finer than Motorola's famous "Golden Voice" tone that's as rich and true as the original sound itself.

Motorola TV

LEADER TODAY BECAUSE OF 25 YEARS OF
PIONEERING IN THE ELECTRONICS INDUSTRY

Chapter Nineteen

Michael Joseph Pallamary Jr., aka Mickey Palmer, was born in Jamaica Plain, MA on May 18, 1922. His father, Michael J. Pallamary Sr., born in Smyrna, Turkey on February 17, 1889, had emigrated to the US via Naples, Italy, aboard the ship Canopic arriving in Boston on October 1, 1907. He worked for a time as an interpreter at Ellis Island and eventually found a job as a waiter at the Copley Plaza Hotel in Boston where he met his future wife, a waitress named Dorothy Madeline Burgee from Norfolk, VA. They wed on June 20, 1915, and settled into the Jamaica Plain section of Boston. Daughter Mildred was born on November 16, 1920 and son Michael J. Pallamary Jr., entered the world on May 18, 1922. Young Mike, called Joey by his doting Mom, loved music and developed a knack for drumming by banging on tables, boxes, and pots and pans. Madeline indulged him and as he grew older she encouraged his musical aspirations.

After graduating from Jamaica Plain High School,

he worked as a drummer booking gigs around town and in outlying areas and on October 28, 1942, he enlisted in the US Navy, assigned to the USS California. While onboard he was responsible for the musical broadcasts and continued his studies as a drummer with the rank of Musician Second Class.

Excerpt from "On the Air" from The Cub, Weekly Newspaper of
The California USS (BB-44):
"Several home-talent programs originated by members of the crew, have proved to be very successful...Mickey Pallamary conducts another program entitled, "News of Your Name Bands" ...But the greatest thrill was the sheer joy of sharing, with great numbers of swell GI guys, the music and fun of the United States of America which we were lucky to have aboard the USS California (BB-44)."

During his service aboard ship he was engaged in several battles. According to military records, he actively participated in the following wartime maneuvers:

UNITED STATES NAVAL SERVICE
MICHAEL J. PALLAMARY

June 11 – Aug. 10, 1944 - *bombardment and occupation of* **SAIPAN**

July 12 – Aug. 15, 1944 - *bombardment and occupation of* **GUAM**

July 20 – Aug. 15, 1944 – *bombardment and*

occupation of **TINIAN**

Oct. 17 – Nov. 20, 1944 – *bombardment and occupation* **LEYTE** *Philippine Islands (received a Philippine Liberation Ribbon for more than 30 days service on USS California and participated in initial landing operations on* **Leyte Island, Philippines** *and engaged enemy surface forces in* **Battle of Surigao Strait***)*

Oct. 24, 1944 – Battle of Surigao Strait *against enemy surface forces, ship was instrumental in destruction of a Japanese Fusō class battleship*

Jan. 4 – Jan. 22, 1945 – *bombardment and occupation from* **LUZON, Philippine Islands (Lingayen Gulf Landings)**

*Jan. 6, 1945 ship hit by kamikaze while providing shore bombardment at Lingayen Gulf. 44 killed and 155 wounded *

Records indicate Mike was granted 30 days of rehabilitation leave, from April 9, 1946 thru March 9, 1946 and while on leave met USO hostess Margaret Regina Moran of Hollywood, MD. He again had 8 days of emergency leave from July 12, 1946 thru July 20, 1946 and finally separated from service on August 16, 1946. On August 31, 1946 he and Margaret Regina married at St. John Church in Hollywood, MD., and he continued to play drums working at the Mammoth Ballroom in South Langhorne, PA. On November 5, 1951, Margaret Regina Pallamary finalized her divorce from Michael while living in Alexandria, VA. He had already left the country by the time she received her divorce decree.

Michael J. Pallamary Jr.
Circa mid 1940's

Mickey Pallamary on drums
Top right beneath O
Inscribed "To the Bestest Mother in the World-
Your Son Joey"
Circa early 1940's

Mickey and his mother Madeline 1943
Photo courtesy of Bob Carr

Chapter Twenty

Many passengers on the flight were virtual strangers, having crowded onto the passenger plane with limited luggage, quickly taking their seats with curt nods to their travel companions in lieu of introductions. Some had never flown before. Their nervousness and anxiety made them excessively chatty or solemnly silent, and most everyone was exhausted. By the time the flight ended publicity opportunities awaited them so the women used small compacts to check their hair, applying ruby red lipstick if needed, while the men slid combs through slickened hair and smoothed wrinkled shirts.

First in line to disembark was theatrical producer Noel Sherman, a Russian emigre from New York who was responsible for hiring and directing the crew in his newest production "Water Capers." While visiting New York, Sherman approached Billy Creedon about working with The Three Rays. After auditioning a variety of performers from drummers to swimmers, a multi-talented troupe was chosen for the international show. The first of many stops in Latin American was Bogota, Columbia.

The tour was exciting. Eager audiences filled nightclubs and theatres to see the beautiful women spin, twirl, and tumble, applauding and cheering each act. On days off the performers became tourists, climbing and crossing over rough terrain to visit ruins and local attractions, relaxing by the hotel pools and cabanas, forming bonds of friendship across the tiled balconies and stucco buildings. Everyone they met was cordial and accommodating which made life pleasant and less stressful, considering they were visitors in a strange country.

Colleen getting ready for takeoff - lower right hand corner

Safe Landing in South America – Colleen center first row

Welcome to South America!

Chapter Twenty-One

During a break in rehearsals one afternoon in Bogota, a weary Colleen stretched out on the wooden stage and closed her eyes. Her legs were sore. She needed new shoes, but the act was going well and they were in demand back home so she counted her blessings and looked on the bright side of things. Focused on her work and the list of upcoming dates, she barely noticed when a man she had seen on the plane sat down on a folding chair near the edge of the stage. After a few moments, drummer Mike Pallamary asked her to join him for a cup of coffee. Weary and needing a break, she welcomed the invitation for caffeine and conversation. They strolled outside to a small café and ordered freshly brewed coffee.

They were both from New England and shared a love of music and theatre. He was 8 years older but the age difference didn't seem to matter. Colleen was flattered by his compliments and enjoyed his stories about jazz bands and the motley musicians he met in his adventures. He was smitten by her innocence and beauty, and that flash of naivete in her light blue eyes. They were far from home and felt at ease with each other.

Before long they were meeting for breakfast and dinner, walking hand in hand or lounging by the pool. Mickey sang to her from balconies of hotels and shouted out "I love you" from the street below as amused locals and guests looked on and cheered. He sent flowers and threw pesos in the air letting everyone know he was the happiest man in the world. Bewildered children and adults scampered across the courtyard catching the manna from heaven tossed from the hands of the *baterista loco (crazy drummer)*.

They spent nearly a month in Bogota and from there went to Medellin, Colombia, then to Cali. They celebrated both Christmas and New Year's together along with the rest of their homesick cast. In mid-January, the show moved to Lima, Peru, and Mickey and Colleen's relationship became more serious. They discussed the future in terms of where and what they would do in the coming months. Billy had several bookings lined up for The Three Rays back in the U.S. so there wouldn't be much down time once they returned home. Mickey's divorce was behind him. He planned to find some lucrative gigs in and around Boston now that he had a Latin American tour to add to his musical resume. His big sister was married with children of her own and his father wanted him to learn the details of private investigation work so he could someday run the family detective agency. There were many choices for a young man who would be turning 30 in a few short weeks and Colleen's career was on track.

The group spent a little over a month in Lima, taking in the sights and sounds of yet another fascinating place. Santiago, Chile, was the next leg of the tour where they stayed from February 15 through March 16, sightseeing, enjoying local foods, laughing and partying with the group.

The tour rolled on into Montevideo, Uruguay where, without notice, the rate of pay decreased for Colleen, Judy, and Grace, making it difficult to meet expenses. After three weeks of reduced pay, Colleen was stunned when her paychecks stopped altogether.

The hardworking cast and crew of *Water Capers* were stranded in the lower part of the South American continent and soon discovered that Noel Sherman was to blame. On top of that, young Colleen found out she was pregnant with Mickey's child.

Colleen and Mike in Peru

Party time! Mike and Colleen right corner

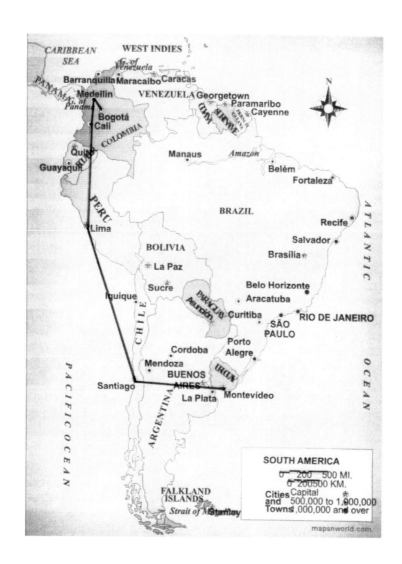

South America Tour Map

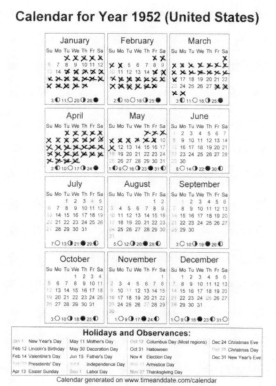

Tour dates in South America
Colleen's earning approximately $829
Average annual income $3850
*** Show Folded May 11, 1952 ***

Chapter Twenty-Two

Noel Sherman did not have a sterling reputation and his questionable business practices drew unwanted attention from several professional organizations including the AGVA. According to newspapers accounts in the August and October, 1946, editions of *The Billboard,* the AGVA intervened in a dispute between Sherman and a club owner when the owner claimed the girls he hired were not only underage, but were not the same girls he had met during negotiations with Sherman. In 1950, he was named as a co-defendant in a propriety rights lawsuit against actor Johnny Weissmuller who was scheduled to appear in Sherman's production called *Watercades.* The unflattering publicity for one of Hollywood's favorite leading men was not appreciated by studio heads.

The revelation that Sherman had absconded with their funds caused panic amongst the incredulous group of Americans stranded in Latin America. Frantic with worry, The Three Rays contacted Billy Creedon in New York to ask for help. Telegrams and letters from the women and their management team flew back and forth and their plight was publicized in *The Billboard* newspaper.

MAY 31, 1952   THE BILLBOARD   GENERAL NEWS

Actor Union Boards Study Merger Plan

Act Stranded In So. America

US Stars Set For Glasgow

Review Index

Highlight Reviews

VAUDEVILLE

Mindy Carson Flashes New Sin Personality, Now Belting 'Em (

By BILL SMITH

TELEVISION

Bertrand Russell, a Thinking M Before a Lens, Could Spark Se

By PAUL ACKERMAN

TELEVISION

WOR's "Nightcap" Has Little I But Horton's Stint Wins Bravos

By SAM CHASE

179

NIGHT CLUBS-VAUDE

16 Communications to 1564 Broadway, New York 36, N. Y. MAY 31, 1952

Water Troupe Stranded in Uruguay; Can't Swim Home

* Continued from page 3

One steamship line offered to bring them back at $200 each but could not pick them up until some time in June.

In the meantime, various cast members had written AGVA complaining they hadn't been paid. Late Wednesday (21) AGVA's National Executive Board authorized Jack Irving, AGVA topper, to deposit the necessary funds in the Montevideo branch of an American bank sufficient to pay the return passage of the performers. It was specifically ordered that these funds would cover only the actors. Sherman, the producer; wardrobe mistresses, if any, or other staff members would not be covered. Early Thursday (22), the American consul at Montevideo, notified Irving by phone that the State Department would pay all return fares, collecting I.O.U.'s. AGVA, in turn, would use its offices to collect from the actors.

AGVA attorneys were studying the documents to see what legal action could be taken against Pan American.

Two Theaters Say They'll

AGVA CRITICISM IS NOW TABOO

NEW YORK, May 26.— Disk jockeys were given notice by the American Guild of Variety Artists that it would not tolerate chatter by deejays on their shows that would reflect on either the union or its officials. The first step was taken against Sam Gyson, doing a nightly deejay platter spinning and confab show over a Miami Beach station.

The complaint was made

Smorgasbord Okay Again—Under Cover

JOEL GREY IS INKED BY COPA

NEW YORK, May 26.— Joel Grey got himself his first big-time cafe break when he auditioned at the Copacabana Wednesday (21) at the midnight show. As a result, he was bought by the Copa for a July date with two options, and will open next week at the Chez Paree, Chicago, on the Jane Fretton show.

Grey is currently in the Warner Brothers' Picture, "About Face." He is the son of Mickey Katz, band leader. Grey's only appearance in New York was last season in "Borscht Capades."

Ill. Supreme Court Upholds

ACCIDENT PLAN LIGHTS ARA, AGVA BOMB

Guild Points to Nix On $1 Payments; Irving Calls Action

NEW YORK, May 26.—A battle between the Artists Representatives Association and the American Guild of Variety Artists is shaping up as a result of the accident insurance program. AGVA has charged ARA with failure to live up to its contract, pointing to agents in Michigan, Illinois and New York, all ARA members, who have flatly refused to pay the $1 per man per show on dates.

The most recent case was with Detroit bookers, Delbridge

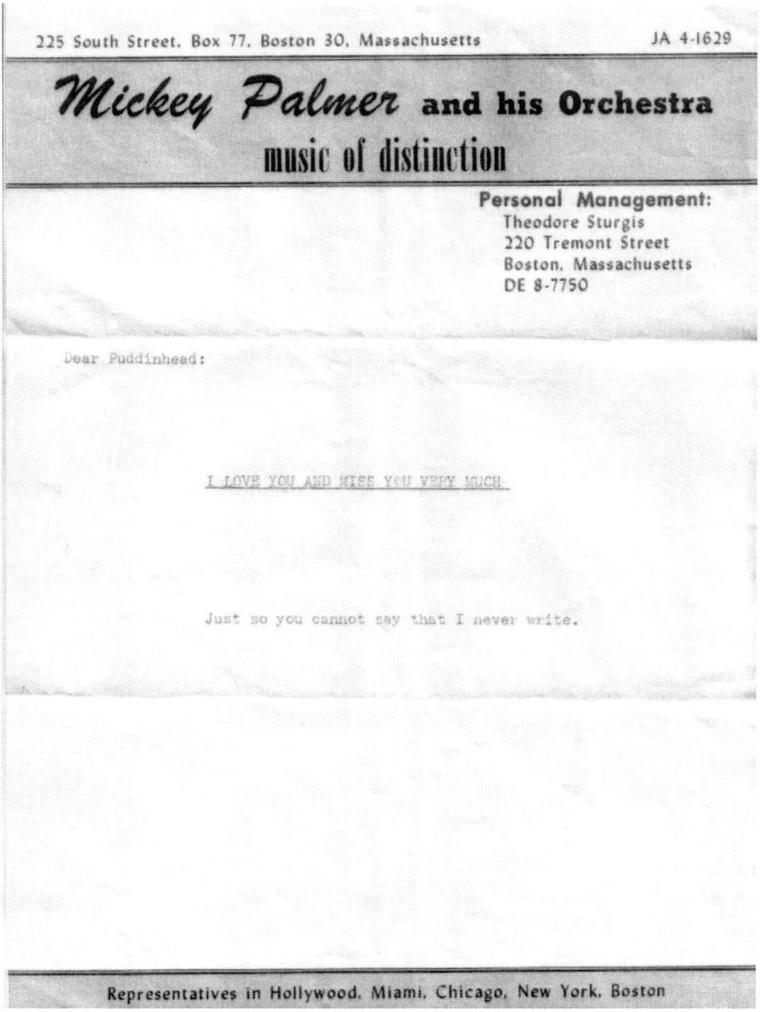

225 South Street, Box 77, Boston 30, Massachusetts   JA 4-1629

Mickey Palmer and his Orchestra
music of distinction

Personal Management:
Theodore Sturgis
220 Tremont Street
Boston, Massachusetts
DE 8-7750

Dear Puddinhead:

I LOVE YOU AND MISS YOU VERY MUCH.

Just so you cannot say that I never write.

Representatives in Hollywood, Miami, Chicago, New York, Boston

Mike's love letter to Colleen

Chapter Twenty-Three

Through numerous sources Creedon learned Sherman was in Italy trying to book acts there in an effort to generate income for himself while leaving everyone else stranded in Uruguay. The AGVA was soon involved as was the US Embassy in Montevideo and the State Department in Washington, D.C. Arranging for accommodations, meals, and other expenses was not easy and neither were the strict guidelines for returning home. Because they were in a foreign country, US citizens had to follow certain protocols in order to arrange transportation and the process of repatriation for indigent people to get back to the United States took time.

The U.S. Repatriation Program, part of the Social Security Act enacted in 1935, was specifically designed to provide temporary assistance to U.S. citizens… "because of destitution, illness, war, threat of war, or a similar crisis, and are without available resources." (excerpt from U.S. Health & Human Services Fact Sheet U.S. Repatriation Program). One of the four components of the program, "emergency repatriation", involved an assessment by the Department of State. In the case of The Three Rays, temporary assistance in the form of a loan repayable to the US government was granted and was good for 90 days.

While the young women dealt with the details of applying for assistance, Pallamary contacted his parents in Massachusetts and planned his return home. He had just learned he was going to be a father and knew his parents would not be pleased when he shared the news of his impending marriage to a "showgirl". Colleen, Gloria, and Judy tried not to panic and relied on each other for both moral and financial support. Colleen's growing waistline was apparent to the others, but she wanted to keep the news of Sherman's theft and her pregnancy from Murph.

With each passing day, a sense of foreboding shadowed their every move. Finally, the paperwork was processed and medical clearances allowed everyone to leave Uruguay. Colleen received a loan of $336.09 from the US State Department to pay for her trip home.

She gripped the armrests as the plane descended into Idlewild Airport at the end of May 1952. She dreaded telling Murph and Frank about her romance and subsequent pregnancy knowing their strict Catholic beliefs and Murph's preoccupation with proper appearances. She rehearsed several scenarios in her mind as the others chattered away in the seats behind her. They all had little satisfaction in knowing the AGVA was actively searching for Noel Sherman who was hopscotching from one country to another trying to avoid anyone associated with his *Water Capers* fiasco.

Mike returned home to Jamaica Plain and found a gig at the Brown Derby in Boston. Neither of his parents were pleased with his plans and tried to dissuade him from marrying "the showgirl". Pallamary Sr. went so far as to offer his son's soon-to-be bride thousands of dollars to just go away. Both parents felt the dancer was beneath their only son.

On July 28, 1952, the young couple applied for a marriage license. Confused and apprehensive, Colleen sought advice from a local priest before marrying Mike and was sorely disappointed when the cleric wished her luck in both her marriage and impending birth.

Faced with fierce opposition from all sides, Michael J. Pallamary Jr., and Colleen J. Bartram exchanged wedding vows on August 10, 1952 in Southbridge, MA. Some two months later, on September 19, 1952, I was born in Bridgeport hospital, a living testament to the love they had found in Lima, Peru. Bridgeport's Sweetheart had a sweetheart of her own and it was time for a final curtain call on the extraordinary career of a gifted performer whose talent and beauty graced the globe entertaining others for nearly two decades.

ABOUT THE AUTHOR

As the eldest child of Colleen Bartram, author Colleen J. Pallamary chronicles her mother's struggle to overcome the crippling effects of rickets as a child to her rise as an international entertainer touring the United States and Latin America in the late 1940's through early 1950's. Based on extensive research, personal scrapbooks, and cherished mother-daughter conversations, *Meet Bridgeport's Sweetheart Colleen J. Bartram* is a loving tribute to her mother's past.

Other books by Ms. Pallamary include *Scammunition: How To Protect Yourself From Con Artists: A Guide For Baby Boomers And Beyond* and an urban fantasy novel titled *The Vampire Preservation Society*. Her books are available on http://www.Amazon.com. She is a speaker, copy editor, freelance writer, and is an American Heart Association Certified BLS Instructor and community volunteer. She is currently working on a sequel to her novel and continues to research the scam phenomenon.

For more information visit:

.http://www.colleenpallamary.com